APORETICS

NICHOLAS RESCHER

Aporetics

Rational
Deliberation
in the
Face of
Inconsistency

UNIVERSITY OF PITTSBURGH PRESS

Published by the University of Pittsburgh Press, Pittsburgh, Pa., 15260
Manufactured in the United States of America
Printed on acid-free paper
10 9 8 7 6 5 4 3 2 1
ISBN 13: 978-0-8229-4363-1
ISBN 10: 0-8229-4363-8

Library of Congress Cataloging-in-Publication Data

Rescher, Nicholas.
    Aporetics : rational deliberation in the face of inconsistency / Nicholas Rescher.
        p.   cm.
    Includes bibliographical references and index.
    ISBN-13: 978-0-8229-4363-1 (cloth : alk. paper)
    ISBN-10: 0-8229-4363-8 (cloth : alk. paper)
  1. Aporia. I. Title.
    B187.A66R47 2009
    121—dc22   2008037727

For my earliest students
Brian Skyrms, Ernest Sosa, James Sterba

CONTENTS

PREFACE

In various books published over the past forty years I have examined various aspects of aporetics—the theory of rational deliberation in the face of inconsistencies. The time has now come to assemble the ideas at issue into a unified overall account that provides a unified a comprehensive and integrated picture of the overall theory and practice of aporetics. The present book addresses this objective of providing treatment of all the separate-seeming issues that manifest the utility, versatility, and power of the aporetic method.

The root idea of aporetics lies in the combination of reductive quality control in situations where we have succumbed to the cognitive overcommitment of inconsistency and find ourselves having to salvage some part of what must be abandoned. It may seem surprising in that this selfsame process of analysis recurs over so diversified a variety of cognitive endeavors. The book nevertheless seeks to synthesize and systematize an aporetic procedure for dealing with information overload (of "cognitive dissonance," as it is sometimes called). What is involved is not a substantive doctrine but a procedural method for analyzing ideas in difficult situations of information management. It turns out that this single method—coherence tropism via plausibility analysis—can be used to deal with issues in many areas of deliberation and information processing, including hypothetical reasoning, inquiry epistemology, paradox analysis, and others. Even some substantial sectors of philosophical dialectic fall naturally within the reach of this methodology. The book endeavors to provide an integrated account of this method together with a set of case studies exhibiting the wider range of its effective applications.

The idea of apories goes back to the puzzling "big questions" of Plato's dialogues. Yet no one made much of this resource as such until Nicolai Hartmann's 1921 *Grundzüge einer Metaphysik der Erkenntnis* (Foundations of a Metaphysic of Knowledge), which viewed apories as difficult foundational questions on the order of "How is it possible to know about not-knowing." Hartmann's ideas found some resonance among German philosophers but became mired in metaphysical stratospherics. The present author's more practical view of apories as arising from actual inconsistencies in our belief inclinations goes back to a series of investigations published in the early 1960s. A survey of the history of the relevant ideas is given in Arto Siitonen's *Problems of Aporetics* (Helsinki: Academia Scieniarum Fennica, 1989).

I am grateful to Estelle Burris for her capable help in preparing this material for publication.

APORETICS

▶1◀

The Nature of Apories

▶What Is an Apory?

In Greek, *aporia* literally means an impasse, a blockage where there is no practicable way to go forward. The word eventually came to characterize any thing, situation—and even person!—who is difficult to deal with. In philosophy, it came to mean a puzzle, a perplexity, an intractable or at least deeply problematic issue. For present purposes, however, the term will be used in a more specific sense to characterize any cognitive situation in which the threat of inconsistency confronts us. Accordingly, an apory will here be understood as a group of individually plausible but collectively incompatible theses.

A word on lexicography. In philosophical discussion, the Greek term *aporia* has been retained. This is a regrettable complication. For ease of usage, the term should be anglicized, along with harmony, symphony, melody, and, indeed, philosophy itself.

Note, for the sake of illustration, the following cluster of contentions constitutes an apory:

1. What the sight of our eyes tells us is to be believed.
2. Sight tells us the stick is bent.
3. What the touch of our hands tells us is to be believed.
4. Touch tells us the stick is straight.

Here each thesis may seem undividedly plausible, but they conjoin to issue in inconsistency. And owing to the contradiction that arises among them, these statements cannot be maintained together. The interests of mere self-consistency require that at least one of them has to be abandoned and replaced—or at least qualified. With apories we thus have not only a collective inconsistency but superadd to this a conception of plausibility that enables us to retain as much information conveyed by the conflicting propositions at issue as the logic of the situation and the cognitive possibilities at hand permit.

Or again concern the following claims:

- Every person has some weight or other.
- The weight of a person is given by a particular mathematical quantity.
- Every particular mathematical quantity is accurate to ten decimal places.
- The weight of a person is accurate to ten decimal places.

Here again, we have individually plausible contentions that are collectively inconsistent. And it is just this that constitutes an apory.

Situations of this aporetic nature arise in very different contexts of application. In addressing cognitive problems we seek to maximize our opportunities by pressing matters to the limits. We thus embark on speculations that not only reach but also overreach, and thereby plunge into inconsistency. This process reflects a general—and understandable—tendency to hypertrophy that manifests itself in many areas as populations or organizations grow to a point that threatens their very viability. And just this is a phenomenon that we encounter in various cognitive contexts; for our inclinations to accept, or to conjecture, and even merely to suppose, often plunge us into inconsistency. Just here is the explanation for the pervasive proliferation of aporetic situations across a varied range of information-management settings.

The resolution of apories calls for a plausibility analysis that enables the chain of inconsistency to be broken at the weakest link. The fact is that any and every apory can be resolved by simply abandoning some (or all) of the commitments whose conjoining creates a contradiction. In principle, the apory management is thus a straightforward process that calls for appraising the comparative plausibility of what we accept, and then restoring consistency by making what is less plausible give way to what is more so. It is this generic and uniform structure of inconsistency management that paves the way to that single overarching discipline of aporetics.[1] The exploration of this domain is the principal task of the present book, whose central thesis is that there indeed is such a general and uniform approach to the rational management of apories.

Use of this aporetic method does not issue in a guarantee of truth. All that the analysis is able to do for us is optimize—that is, to maximize plausibility via considerations of systemic coherence in matters of question-resolution. Aporetics is thus less a method of innovation than of regimentation: its task is not to engender new insights but to bring systemic order and coherence into those we already have. In Leibnizian terms, it is not an *ars inveniedi* but an *ars componendi*.

▶ *What Does Confronting an Apory Require?*

The prime directive of cognitive rationality is to maintain consistency and consequently to restore consistency to inconsistent situations. To be sure, it is a *possible* reaction to paradox simply to take contradictions in stride. With Pascal, we might accept contradictions for the sake of greater interests and say that "à la fin de chacque vérité, il faut ajouter qu'on se souvient de la verité opposée" (after every truth one must be mindful of the opposite truth).[2] The Greek philosopher

Protagoras (b. ca. 480 B.C.), the founding father of the Sophistic school,[3] notoriously held that the human situation was in this way paradoxical throughout, and that *anything and everything* that we believed could be argued for *pro* and *con* with equal cogency.[4] But this sort of resignation in the face of inconsistency is hardly a comfortable—let alone a rational—posture. Even if one's sympathies are so inordinately wide, inconsistency tolerance should be viewed as a position of last resort, to be adopted only after all else has failed us.[5] For once consistency is lost, how is it to be regained?

When confronted with an apory there is no rationally viable alternative to rejecting one or more of the theses involved, since accepting all results in inconsistency. Here our cognitive sympathies have become overextended, and we must make some curtailment in the fabric of our commitments. So doing nothing is not a rationally viable option when we are confronted with a situation of aporetic inconsistency. Something has to give: some one (at least) of those incompatible contentions at issue must be abandoned. Apories constitute situations of *forced choice* among the alternative contentions.

Consider a historical example drawn from the Greek theory of virtue:

1. If virtuous action does not produce happiness (pleasure) then it is motivationally impotent and generally pointless.

2. Virtue in action is eminently pointful and should provide a powerfully motivating incentive.

3. Virtuous action does not always—and perhaps not even generally—produce happiness (pleasure).

It is clearly impossible—on grounds of mere logic alone—to maintain this family of contentions. At least one member of the group must be abandoned.

But of course if we are going to be sensible about it, we will be under the rational obligation to provide some sort of account—some rationale—to justify this step. Whatever particular exit from inconsistency we adopt will have to be accompanied by a story of science, and that justifies this step. And so with the preceding virtue illustration we face the choice among the following alternatives:

1. Abandonment: Maintain that virtue has substantial worth quite on its own account, even if it does not produce happiness or pleasure (Stoicism, Epictetus, Marcus Aurelius).

2. Abandonment: Dismiss virtue as ultimately unfounded and unrationalizable, viewing morality as merely a matter of the customs of the country (Sextus Empiricus) or the will of the rulers (Plato's Thrasymachus).

3. Abandonment: Insist that virtuous action does indeed always yield happiness or pleasure—at any rate to the right-minded. Virtuous action is inherently pleasure producing for fully rational agents, so that the virtue and happiness are inseparably interconnected (Plato, the Epicureans).

When an apory confronts us, a forced choice among the propositions involved becomes unavoidable. We cannot maintain the status quo but must, one way or another, "take a position"—some particular thesis must be abandoned as it stands.

There Are Always Multiple Exits from Aporetic Inconsistency

There are always alternatives for removing aporetic inconsistency by curtailments. It lies in the logical nature of things that there will always be multiple exits from aporetic inconsistency. For whenever such conflicting contentions confront us, then no matter which particular resolution we ourselves may favor, and no matter how firmly we are persuaded of its merits, the fact remains that there will also be other, alternative ways of resolving the inconsistency. For a contradiction that arises from overcommitment can always be averted by abandoning different candidates among the conflicting contentions, so that distinct awareness to averting inconsistency can always be found. Strict logic alone dictates only *that* something must be abandoned; it does not indicate what. No particular resolutions are imposed by abstract rationality alone—by the mere "logic of the situation." (In philosophical argumentation one person's *modus ponens* is another's *modus tollens*.) It is always a matter of trade-offs, of negotiation, of giving up a bit of this in order to retain a bit of that. Accordingly, aporetics is not only a matter of logic but calls for good judgment as well. Thus consider the following aporetic cluster:

1. Some facts can be explained satisfactorily.
2. No explanation of a fact is (fully) satisfactory when it involves unexplained facts.
3. Any satisfactory explanation must be noncircular: it must always involve some *further* facts (facts distinct from the fact that is being explained) to provide materials for its explanatory work.

Premise 3 indicates the need for unexplained explainers. Premise 2 asserts that the presence of unexplained explainers prevents explanations from being satisfactory. Together they entail that there are no (fully) satisfactory explanations. But premise 1 insists that satisfactory explanations exist. And so we face a contradiction. A forced choice among a fixed spectrum of alternatives confronts us. And there are just three exits from this inconsistency:

1. Abandonment: Explanatory skepticism. Forgo the explanatory project altogether.
2. Abandonment: Explanatory foundationalism. Insist that some facts are obvious or self-evident in a way that exempts them from any need for being explained themselves and make them available as "cost-free" inputs for the explanation of other facts.
3. Abandonment: Explanatory coherentism. Accept circular explanations as adequate in some cases ("very large circles").

We have the prospect of alternative resolutions—but over a well-defined spectrum of alternatives. The range of choice before us is limited.

As such examples show, any particular resolution of an aporetic cluster is bound to be simply *one possibility among others.* The single most crucial fact about an aporetic cluster is that there will always be a variety of distinct ways of averting the inconsistency into which it plunges us. We are not just forced to choose, but specifically constrained to operate within a narrowly circumscribed range of choice.

The theory of morality developed in Greek ethical thought affords a good example of such an aporetic situation. Greek moral thinking is inclined to view that the distinction between right and wrong:

1. Does matter

2. Is based on custom (*nomos*)

3. Can only matter if grounded in the objective nature of things (*phusei*) rather than in mere custom

Here, too, an aporetic problem arises. The inconsistency of these contentions led to the following resolutions:

1. Deny: Issues of right and wrong just do not matter—they are a mere question of power, of who gets to "lay down the law" (Thrasymachus).

2. Deny: The difference between right and wrong is not a matter of custom but resides in the nature of things (Stoics).

3. Deny: The difference between right and wrong is only customary (*nomoi*) but does really matter all the same (Heracleitus).

We have here a paradigmatic example of an antinomy: a *theme* provided by an aporetic cluster of propositions, with *variations* set by the various ways of resolving this inconsistency. There will always be alternatives here since the objective of consistency resolution is something which, in principle, can always be accomplished in very different ways.

The Mission of Aporetics

When confronted with an aporetic situation, we of course can, in theory, simply throw up our hands and abandon the *entire* cluster of theses involved. But this total suspension of judgment is too great a price to pay. In taking this course of wholesale abandonment, we would plunge into vacuity by foregoing answers to too many questions. We would curtail our information not only beyond necessity but beyond comfort as well, seeing that we have some degree of commitment to all members of the cluster and do not want to abandon more of them than we have to. Our best option—or only sensible option—is to try to localize the difficulty in order to save what we can. In this way aporetics is, in effect, a venture in cognitive damage control in the face of inconsistencies.

The mission of aporetics is thus to provide a practicable means for coming to terms with inconsistency. Particularly prominent among the situations in which inconsistency arises are:

- Conflicting information that arises from discordant sources in matters of empirical inquiry
- Conflicts that arise when new information disagrees with the old
- Conflicts of putative fact with speculative supposition in thought experimentation and hypothetical reasoning, counterfactual conditionalization, and *ad absurdum* and *per impossible* reasoning
- Paradoxes in matters of theoretical deliberations where some of our belief-inclinations disagree with others in speculative conjecture regarding history
- Conflicts arising in philosophy through the clash of doctrines and contentions

The ensuing deliberations will address all of these issues.

2

Coherentism

AN APORETIC APPROACH
TO EMPIRICAL INQUIRY

The Ways of Inconsistency

An acknowledgment of contradictions in nature goes back to the pre-Socratics.[1] And if not Hegel himself, then at any rate many of his followers maintained the realization of contradictions in the world.[2] Marxists of various sorts have more recently been strident supporters of such a view. It is a major historic position that merits careful evaluation.

Consistency is unquestionably a prime desideratum in inquiry, but there is nothing guaranteed about it. Individually plausible contentions often disagree with one another. As the ancient sceptics stressed, experience confronts us with an inconsistent world: sight tells us the stick held at an angle underwater is bent; touch tells us it is straight. Each eye presents a somewhat different picture of the world: the brain alone enables us to "see" it consistently. To assert the consistency of nature as we grasp it is to express one's faith that the mind will be able ultimately to impress theoretical consistency upon experienced complexity. But this confidence may in the final analysis prove to be misplaced. It is at best a *hope* that all such *apparent* discords are merely that and admit of ultimate reconciliation, a hope for whose realization a good deal of theorizing is required. And there is no reason of a priori general principle to think that this will always prevail at any and every stage of inquiry—that we might in fact not always be able to propel the state of theorizing to a point where all awkward conflicts admit of smooth theoretical reconciliation. After all, theorizing itself involves speculation and is thereby also open to inconsistency. Overall, the risk of inconsistency is an ineliminable fact of epistemic life. Its shadow dogs every step of the quest for "a true picture of reality." Every theoretical extrapolation from the data runs the risk of clashing head-on with some other. The data themselves may conflict and cry out for theoretical reconciliation. After all, error avoidance is not the be-all and end-all of the cognitive enterprise: "Seek truth!" is no less important an injunction than "Avoid error!" and these two desiderata stand in inextricable interrelation: the prospect of truth itself unavoidably carries with it the risk of error—and even inconsistency. There is nothing regrettable, and nothing irrational, about adopting epistemic policies that allow occasional errors—*and even inconsistencies*—to slip through the net, provided that the general quality of the catch is high enough.

The overall synthesis of our knowledge (i.e., what we *think* we know) with our metaknowledge (our knowledge about this knowledge) affords an interesting illustration of the impetus toward inconsistency. The so-called Preface Paradox formulated by D. C. Makinson affords a vivid view of this phenomenon:

> Consider "the writer who, in the Preface to his book, concedes the occurrence of errors among his statements. Suppose that in the course of his book a writer makes a great many assertions, which we shall call $S_1, \ldots, S_n$. Given each

one of these, he believes that it is true. . . . However, to say that not everything I assert in this book is true, is to say that at least one statement in this book is false. That is to say that at least one of $S_1, \ldots, S_n$ is false, where $S_1, \ldots, S_n$ are the statements in the book; that $(S_1 \& \ldots \& S_n)$ is false; that $\sim(S_1 \& \ldots \& S_n)$ is true. The author who writes and believes each of $S_1 \ldots, S_n$ and yet in a preface asserts and believes $\sim(S_1 \& \ldots \& S_n)$ is, it appears, behaving very rationally. Yet clearly he is holding logically incompatible beliefs: he believes each of $S_1, \ldots, S_n, \sim(S_1 \& \ldots \& S_n)$, which form an inconsistent set. The author is being rational though inconsistent.[3]

We begin with the series of statements in the text or main body of the book: $S_1, S_2, \ldots, S_n$. (For simplicity and convenience we shall suppose that there are just two of these, i.e., $n = 2$.) Now the preface maintains that not all of these are true: $\sim(S_1 \& S_2)$. The resulting overall assertion-set $\{S_1, S_2, \sim(S_1 \& S_2)\}$ is clearly inconsistent. Nevertheless, there is a strong impetus to accepting the whole of this set, and the tendency of this impetus is by no means irrational.

In this connection, Keith Lehrer has written:

The addition of such a [preface paradoxical] belief is not worth the loss measured in terms of the objective of believing *only* what is true. . . . He has purchased the certainty of having one true belief at the price of ensuring that he has one false belief. The price is even more dear. By adding the belief which renders his beliefs inconsistent he automatically forgoes the chance of optimum success in the search for truth, that is, believing truths and only truths.[4]

But this is quite unrealistic. The epistemic *ideal* calls not just for accepting *only* truths, but for accepting *all* truths. Error avoidance itself can prove part of that best which is the enemy of the good. For in inquiry we should strive not just to avoid falsity but to engross truth. The name of the epistemic game is not the attainment of some transcendent ideal but the achievement of the best realizable balance of truth over falsity. And here the practical politics of the situation may well enjoin the toleration of inconsistency upon us.

As William James forcibly emphasized, the aim of the cognitive enterprise is not just to avoid error but also to engross truth. To secure truths we must *accept* something: nothing ventured, nothing gained! And to accept something rationally, we must have rules or standards of acceptance. But if these rules or standards indicate the acceptability of mutually discordant theses (as they indeed can), then there is something unsatisfying—something too pristine, purist, and persnickety—about rejecting them en bloc simply and solely on this account. To be sure, no sensible person would court inconsistency for its own sake. But this is not the issue. The point is that one can reasonably be in a position of deeming inconsistencies plausible when driven to it by the operation of (otherwise defensible) acceptance principles. The very drive toward *completeness*—itself a key parameter of systematic adequacy—can and does so operate as to enjoin at least temporary and provisional inconsistency toleration upon us.

But of course when inconsistency looms we can no longer view what we have as truths. They will at best be truth candidates or *plausible data*, as we shall here call them. And the move from plausible datahood to presumptive truth is always something that requires epistemic work and effort to overcome the inconsistencies at issue. It is here that the wheels of the mill of aporetics will begin to grind.

▶ The Key Concept of a Datum

The key to dealing with inconsistency in inquiry lies in treating those incompatible materials not as established *truths*, but as provisional *data*. And just this affords the means by which aporetics gains its hold in factual inquiry.

The concept of a *datum*, whose role is pivotal in coherentist methodology, is something of a technical resource. To be sure, the idea is one not *entirely* unrelated to the ordinary use of that term, nor to its (somewhat different) use among philosophers; yet it is significantly different from both. A datum is a plausible *truth candidate*, a proposition to be taken not as true, but as potentially or *presumptively* true. It is a prima facie truth in exactly the sense in which one speaks of prima facie duties in ethics—a thesis that we would in these circumstances be prepared to class as true provided that no countervailing considerations are operative. A datum is thus a proposition that one is to class as true *if one can*, that is, if doing so does not generate any difficulties or inconsistencies. It is not *established* as true, but is backed only by the *presumption* of being likely to turn out true if all goes well. It lays a claim to truth, but it may not be able to make good this claim in the final analysis. A datum is not so much a "given" as a "taken." But a proposition may be *taken* in two ways:

> *For good and all as a truth*—as *actually true*; to be definitively classed as true

and

> *On approval* as a *truth candidate* or as *potentially or presumptively true*; to be classed as true provisionally—that is, provided that doing so creates no problems or anomalies

Now a presumption is a proposition that is "taken" not in the first, unqualified mode, but only in the second: it is a surrogate truth—a *claimant* or *pretender* to truth whose credentials may in the end prove insufficient, a runner in a race it may not win.

The "acceptance" of a proposition as a truth candidate is not outright *acceptance* at all but a highly provisional and conditional epistemic *inclination* toward it, an inclination that falls far short of outright commitment. As far as their truthfulness is concerned, data are not *givens* but *takens*.

Viewed as such, a datum is a cognitive presumption—no more than a putative truth, accepted tentatively as a claim that one is to class as true *if one can*—that is, if doing so generates no difficulties or inconsistencies. The starting of a presumption is provisioned: it is not *established* as true, it is backed only by a rationally warranted expectation that it may turn out true "if all goes well." It is a prima facie truth in exactly the sense in which one speaks of prima facie duties in ethics. A prima facie "duty" amounts to an actual duty only provided that no countervailing conditions are operative. Similarly, a presumption is a prima facie "truth" in that the evidentiations are sufficiently positive that we are under the circumstances prepared to class it as *actually true* provided that no countervailing considerations are operative. It lays a claim to truth, but it may not be able to make good this claim in the final analysis. But a claim to truth—even one that is advanced hesitatingly and provisionally—is still just that, namely a claim to *truth*. And it would be altogether wrong to equate a tentative claim to truth with a claim to tentative truth! They are every bit as different as a hesitant confession of wrongdoing differs from a confession of hesitant wrongdoing. The fact that a claim to truth is provisional does not render it a claim to provisional truth.

This distinction between certified truths and merely presumptive truth candidates demands emphasis because it is central to present purposes. Any *experiential* justification of a truth criterion must pull itself up by its own bootstraps—it needs factual inputs, but yet these factual inputs cannot at this stage already qualify as truths. To meet this need, it is natural to appeal to truth candidates, data which are no more certified *truths* than presidential candidates are certified presidents—though some of them are ultimately bound to win out. All the same, to class a proposition as a datum is to take a definite and committal position with respect to it, so as to say, "I propose to accept it as true insofar as this is permitted by analogous and possibly conflicting commitments elsewhere."

The concept of the datahood is the crux of a coherentist approach to truth. It serves to provide an answer to the question "Coherent with what?" without postulating a prior category of fundamental truth. It provides the coherence theory with grist to its mill that need not itself be the product of some preliminary determinations of truth. A reliance upon data makes it possible to contemplate a coherence theory that produces truth not ex nihilo (which would be impossible), but from a basis that does not itself demand any prior determinations of truthfulness as such. A coherence criterion can, on this basis, furnish a mechanism that is *originative* of truth—that is, it yields truths as outputs without requiring that truths must also be present among the supplied inputs.

What is clearly needed for a viable coherence epistemology is a halfway house between coherence with *some*—that is, *any*—propositions (which would be trivial) and coherence with *true* propositions (which would be circular with a criterion for truth). Essentially, what is needed is coherence with somehow "the right" propositions. The coherence at issue in a coherence theory of truth must be construed as involving all in some way *appropriately qualified* propositions. This line of thought poses a task central to the construction of a workable coherence theory: that of specifying just what propositions are at stake when one speaks of determining the truth of a given proposition in terms of its "coherence *with others*." Which others are at issue? It was, of course, for the sake of a satisfactory answer to this question that our approach made its crucial resort to the key concept of an experientially grounded *datum* that here concerns us.

It is sometimes objected that coherence cannot be the standard of truth because there we may well arrive at a multiplicity of diverse but equally coherent structures, whereas truth is of its very nature conceived of as unique and monolithic. Bertrand Russell, for example, once argued as follows:

> There is no reason to suppose that only *one* coherent body of beliefs is possible. It may be that, with sufficient imagination, a novelist might invent a past for the world that would per-

fectly fit on to what we know, and yet be quite different from the real past. In more scientific matters, it is certain that there are often two or more hypotheses which account for all the known facts on some subject, and although, in such cases, men of science endeavor to find facts which will rule out all the hypotheses except one, there is no reason why they should always succeed.[5]

One must certainly grant Russell's central point: however the idea of coherence is articulated in the abstract, there is something fundamentally undiscriminating about coherence taken by itself. Coherence may well be—nay certainly is—a descriptive feature of the domain of truths: they cohere. But there is nothing in this to prevent propositions other than truths from cohering with one another: Fiction can be made as coherent as fact; truths surely have no monopoly of coherence. Indeed, it is logically possible to have two different but equally comprehensive sets of coherent statements between which there would be, in the coherence theory, no way to decide which was the set of true statements. In consequence, coherence cannot of and by itself discriminate between truths and falsehoods. Coherence is thus seemingly disqualified as a means for *identifying* truths. Any viable coherence theory of truth must make good the claim that despite these patent facts considerations of coherence can—somehow—be deployed to serve as an indicator of truth.

But the presently envisioned theory averts these difficulties. For one thing it deploys coherence not as a theory of the meaning of truth but as an instrumentality of inquiry. Moreover, it looks not to coherence in and of itself as a criterion of truth, but to coherence with the data of experience. It thus renders Russell's objection effectively irrelevant.

▶ *Examples of Data*

Understanding that data are *potential* truths or truth candidates, the question remains: what procedure is to be used in qualifying a prop-

DISPLAY 2.1. Some rules of cognitive presumption

In the absence of specific indications to the contrary:

- Believe the evidence of your own senses.

- Accept at face value the declarations of other people.

- Accept the determinacy of such standard sources of information as the senses and memory.

- Accept the declarations of recognized experts and authorities within the area of their expertise.

- Trust in the reliability of the standardly employed cognitive aids and instruments (telescopes, calculating machines, reference works, logarithmic tables, etc.).

- Accept those answers to your questions for which the available evidence speaks most strongly.

osition for datahood? What qualifies a contention as presumptively true?

A tradition in philosophical epistemology that reaches from the later Stoics and Academic Sceptics of antiquity to the British Idealists of the turn of the current century insist (not always *expressis verbis*, but in effect) on a presumption of truth in favor of the deliverances of memory and of the senses. Theses based on observation or recollection are to have the benefit of doubt, a presumption of truth in their favor—they are to stand unless significant counterindications are forthcoming. Moreover, we standardly operate with a good many other rules of cognitive presumption, some of the most important of them being listed in display 2.1.

To be sure, one can deploy all of the traditional arguments of the sceptics against the claims of the senses or of memory automatically to afford the truth. After all, we have before us the admonition of Descartes: "All that up to the present time I have accepted as most true and certain I have learned either from the senses or through the senses; but it is sometimes proved to me that these senses are deceptive, and it is wiser not to trust entirely to any thing by which we have once been deceived."[6] But, of course, any such sceptical dismissal of the potential of sensory data serves only to reemphasize their role as presumptions—provisionally acceptable truth claims in our presumptive sense, rather than outright *truths* as such.[7] They represent contentions that merit being accepted as true provisionally, "until further notice," until the path to acceptance is clear, in that the crucial issue that "remains to be seen" has been clarified—namely, whether the presumptive truth will in fact stand up once "everything is said and done."

A further key instance of cognitive presumption is afforded by sources that we can reasonably take to be reliable and which, for that very reason, yield information that we can also reasonably accept. This occurs with particular prominence in the context of expertise and authoritativeness. In recognizing people as experts or authorities in a certain field, we presume that this individual "knows what they are talking about." This presumption in turn authorizes us to suppose that when a well-informed individual states a claim, this may reasonably be assumed to be true. The presumption that underwrites the credibility of expert and authoritative sources is a prime instance of this phenomenon. And this holds not only for "experts" and people we can expect to be "in the know," but also for such impersonal sources of information as instruments or inferential processes. Thus one cannot only presume that the information afforded by an encyclopedia is correct (having presumably been written by experts).

A cognitive presumption stakes a claim that outruns the substance of actually available information; it is a cognitive presumption that is a proposition that, in suitably favorable circumstances, is accepted as true in the absence of any counterindications. This is a default position, as it were, affording an answer to some question of ours that we adopt for lack of anything better and will keep in place until such time as something further comes along that is able to eject it from this position of favor. In this way, cognitive presumptions function as instrumentalities of rational economy. Thanks to them we need not the benefit of answers to our questions until such time as all of the relevant returns are in—which is to say virtually never.

▶Presumption and Plausibility

Plausibilities are thus one thing and truths another. We "accept" plausible statements only tentatively and provisionally, subject to their proving unproblematic in our deliberations. Of course, problems do often arise. X says twenty-five people were present; Y says fifteen. Sight tells us that the stick held at an angle underwater is bent; touch tells us that it is straight. The hand that has been held in cold water indicates that the tepid liquid is warm, but that which has been held in hot water indicates that it is cold. In such cases we cannot have it both ways. Where our sources of information conflict— where they point to aporetically inconsistent conclusions—we can no longer accept their deliverances at face value but must somehow intervene to straighten things out. And here plausibility has to be our guide, subject to the idea that the most plausible prospect has a favorable presumption on its side.

The reason for the prominence of presumption in matters of cognition is straightforward. As beings who must act to live and who guide their creators by their beliefs, we members of *Homo sapiens* have questions and need answers. But in this life we have few categorical guarantees. Where are the truths of seventeenth-century science, and what will our truths be in the year 3000? If the business of presumption did not already have a place in our cognitive arsenal, it would have to be invented. And indeed it was!

Presumptions can be either concrete and specific or abstract and generic. That long-lost individuals are dead is a generic presumption; that Smith who has been missing for many years is dead is a specific presumption. The former is a general rule, the latter a specific application thereof. However, generic presumptions are fundamental. Any acceptable specific presumption must be based on an appropriate generic presumption as an instance thereof. Thus I presume that Dr. X is a qualified medical practitioner because he was listed as such in the yellow pages of the telephone directory. And I presume that his diagnosis of my ailment is correct because I accept him (via the previous presumption) to be a qualified physician. Presumptions, like Shakespearean troubles, come not as single spies but in battalions, with specific presumptions invariably grounded in generic principles.[8]

The plausibility of contentions may also, however, be based not only on a thesis-warranting *source or evidentiation* but also on a thesis-warranting *principle*. Here inductive considerations may come prominently into play; in particular, such warranting principles are the standard inductive desiderata: simplicity, uniformity, specificity, definiteness, determinativeness, "naturalness," etc. With such an approach, one would say that the more simple, the more uniform, the more specific a thesis—either internally, of itself, or externally, in relation to some stipulated basis—the more emphatically this thesis is to count as plausible. Accordingly, the concept of *simplicity* affords a crucial entry point for plausibility considerations. The injunction "Other things being anything like equal, give precedence to simpler hypotheses vis-à-vis more complex ones" can reasonably be espoused as a procedural, regulative principle of presumption, rather than a metaphysical claim as to "the simplicity of nature." On such an approach, we espouse not the Scholastic adage "Simplicity is the sign of truth" (*simplex sigilium veri*), but its cousin, the precept "Simplicity is the sign of plausibility" (*simplex sigilium plausibili*). In adopting this policy we shift the discussion from the plane of the constitutive/descriptive/ontological to that of the regulative/methodological/prescriptive.

Again, uniformity can also serve as a plausibilistic guide to reasoning. Thus consider the Uniformity Principle: In the absence of explicit counterindications, a thesis about unscrutinized cases that conforms to a patterned uniformity obtaining among the data at our disposal with respect to scrutinized cases—a uniformity that is in fact present throughout these data—is more plausible than any of its regularity-discordant contraries. And the more extensive this pattern conformity, the more highly plausible the thesis.

This principle is tantamount to the stance that when the initially given evidence exhibits a marked logical pattern, then pattern-concordant claims relative to this evidence are—*ceteris paribus*—to be evaluated as more plausible than pattern-discordant ones (and the more comprehensively pattern accordant, the more highly plausible). This rule implements the guiding idea of the familiar practice of judging the plausibility of theories and theses on the basis of a "sufficiently close analogy" with otherwise validated cases.[9] (The uniformity principle thus forges a special role for the prioritization of *normality*—of "the usual course of things"—in plausibility assessment.)[10]

In general, the more plausible a thesis, the more smoothly it is consistent and consonant with the rest of our knowledge of the matters at issue. Ordinarily, the removal of a highly plausible thesis from the framework of cognitive commitments would cause a virtual earthquake; removal of a highly implausible one would cause scarcely a tremor; in between we have to do with varying degrees of readjustment and realignment. And in general, then, the closer its fit and the smoother its consonance with our cognitive commitments, the more highly plausible the thesis. Systemic interconnectedness and plausibility thus go hand in hand in a way that renders presumption a key factor in inductive reasoning.[11]

The Coherentist Approach to Inquiry

In general terms, the coherence criterion of truth operates as follows. One begins with a datum set of suitably "given" propositions. These data are not necessarily true *nor yet even consistent*. They are not given as secure truths, in a foundationalist's manner of theses established once and for all, but merely as *presumptive* or *potential* truths—that is, as plausible truth *candidates*—and in general as *competing* ones that are mutually inconsistent. The task to which a coherentist epistemology addresses itself is that of resolving order to dissonant data by separating the sheep from the goats, distinguishing what merits acceptance as true from what does not.

To the criticism why should mere coherence imply truth, one should offer the reply that what is at issue here is not *mere* coherence, but coherence *with the data*. It is not with bare coherence as such (whatever that would be) but with data-directed coherence that a truth-making capacity enters upon the scene. But, of course, this basis of datahood is only a foundation for truth, not the structure itself. What coherence is asked to do is not to establish truth as such but to provide a ground for acceptance as true. It functions not at the ontological but at the epistemic level. Coherence plays this essential role because it is to be through the mediation of coherence considerations that we move from truth candidacy and presumptions of factuality to truth as such. And the procedure is fundamentally noncircular: we need make no imputations of truth at the level of data to arrive at truths through application of the criterial machinery in view.

A coherentist epistemology thus views the extraction of knowledge from the plausible data by means of an analysis of best-fit considerations. Its approach is fundamentally holistic in judging the acceptability of every purported item of information by its capacity to contribute toward a well-ordered, systemic whole.

The procedure at issue with such a coherence analysis accordingly calls for the following epistemic resources:

1. *Data*: theses that can serve as *acceptance candidates* in the context of the inquiry, plausible contentions which, at best, are merely *presumptively* true (like the "data of sense"). These

are not certified truths (or even probable truths) but theses that are in a position to make some claims upon us for acceptance. They are prima facie truths in the sense that we would be prepared to grant them acceptance as true *if* (and this is a very big if) there were no countervailing considerations upon the scene. (The classical examples of "data" in this sense are those of perception and memory.)

2. Plausibility ratings: comparative evaluations of our initial assessment (in the context of issue) of the relative acceptability of the "data." This is a matter of their relative acceptability "at first glance" (so to speak) and *in the first analysis*, prior to their systematic evaluation. The plausibility standing of truth candidates is thus to be accorded without any prejudgments as to how these theses will fare *in the final analysis*.

Accordingly, the general strategy of the coherence theory lies in a three-step procedure: (1) to gather in all of the relevant "data" (in the present technical sense of this term); (2) to inventory the available conflict-resolving options that represent the alternative possibilities for achieving overall consistency; (3) to choose among these alternatives by using the guidance of plausibility considerations, subject to the principle of minimizing implausibility. In the face of aporetic inconsistency, the coherence theory implements F. H. Bradley's dictum that *system* (i.e., systematicity) provides a test criterion most appropriately fitted to serve as arbiter of truth. And in this basis, mutual coherence becomes the arbiter of acceptability which make the less plausible alternatives give way to those of greater plausibility. The acceptability-determining mechanism at issue proceeds on the principle of optimizing our admission of the claims implicit in the data, striving to maximize our retention of the data subject to the plausibilities of the situation. The process of deriving useful information from imperfect data is a key feature of the coherence theory of truth, which faces, rather than evades (like standard logic), the question of the inferences appropriately to be drawn from an inconsistent set of premises. On this basis, the coherence theory of truth views the problem of truth determination as a matter of bringing order into a chaos comprised of initial data that mingle the secure and the infirm. It sees the problem in transformational terms: incoherence into coherence, disorder into system, candidate truths into qualified truths.

The interaction of observation and theory provides an illustration. Take grammar. Here one moves inferentially from the phenomena of actual usage to the framework of rules by the way of a best-fit principle (an inference to the best systematization, as it were), and one checks that the cycle closes by moving back again to the phenomena by way of their subsumption under the inferred rules. Something may well get lost en route in this process of mutual attunement—for example, some of the observed phenomena of actual language use may simply be dismissed (say as slips of the tongue). Again, the fitting of curves to observation points in scientific theorizing also illustrates this sort of feedback process of discriminating the true and the false on best-fit considerations. The crucial point for present purposes is simply that a systematization can effectively control and correct data—even (to a substantial extent) the very data on which it itself is based.

The coherentist criterion accordingly assumes an entirely *inward* orientation. It does not seek to compare the truth candidates directly with "the facts" obtaining outside the epistemic context. Rather, having gathered in as much information (and this will include also *misinformation*) about the facts as possible—to set on the data, in sum—it seeks to sift the true from the false *within* this body. On the coherentist's theory, justification is thus not a matter of derivation but one of systematization. We operate, in effect, with the question as "justified" = "systematized." The coherence analysis can be thought of as representing, in effect, a systems-analysis approach to the criteriology of truth.

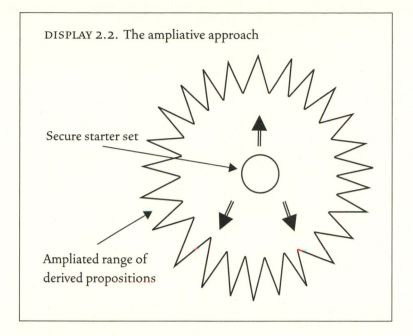

DISPLAY 2.2. The ampliative approach

Secure starter set

Ampliated range of
derived propositions

There are two profoundly different approaches to the cognitive enterprise that, for want of better choices, might be called the *ampliative*
and the *reductive*. The ampliative strategy searches for highly secure
propositions that are acceptable as true beyond reasonable doubt.
Given such a carefully circumscribed and tightly controlled starter
set of propositions, one proceeds to move outward ampliatively by
making inferences from this secure starter set. The resulting picture
is illustrated by display 2.2. Here we proceed expansively, by moving outward from the secure home base of an entirely unproblematic
core.

The reductive strategy, however, proceeds in exactly the opposite
direction. It begins in a quest not for unproblematically acceptable
truths, but for well-qualified candidates or prospects for truth. At
the outset one does not require contentions that are certain and alto-

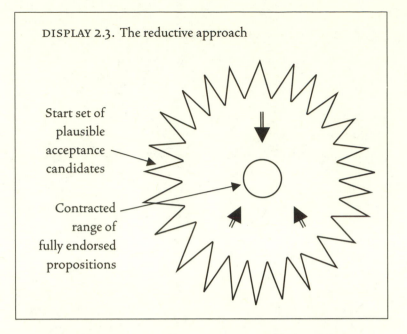

DISPLAY 2.3. The reductive approach

Start set of plausible acceptance candidates

Contracted range of fully endorsed propositions

gether qualified for recognition as genuine truths, but propositions that are no more than plausible, well-spoken-for, well-grounded candidates for endorsement. Of course, not all of these promising truth candidates are endorsed or accepted as true. We cannot simply adopt the whole lot, because they are competing—mutually contradictory. What we have to do is to impose a delimiting (and consistency-restoring) screening out that separates the sheep from the goats until we are left with something that merits endorsement. And here we proceed by way of diminution or compression as per display 2.3, which makes it clear that the reductive approach proceeds by *narrowing* that overample range of plausible prospects for endorsement.

While the paradigm instrument of ampliative reasoning is *deductive* derivation, the paradigm method of contraction is dialectical argumentation. To effect the necessary reductions we do not proceed via a single deductive chain, but through backing and filling along complex cycles which crisscross over the same ground from different angles of approach in their efforts to identify weak spots. The object of the exercise is to determine how well enmeshed a thesis is in the complex fabric of diverse and potentially discordant and competing contentions. We are now looking for the best candidates among competing alternatives—for that resolution for which, on balance, the strongest overall case can be made out. It is not the uniquely correct answer but the most defensible position that we seek in dialectics.

The epistemology of a reductively developed cognitive discipline is thus something radically different from that of an ampliatively developed one. With ampliative reasoning we proceed "foundationally" in the manner of an axiomatic approach. The first and paramount task is to obtain that "starter set"—that firm basis of secure, certain, and unquestionably acceptable propositions from which the rest of the system can be ampliated. We embark on a quest reminiscent of Descartes for clear and distinct certainties on whose basis we can erect a larger cognitive structure. Security, certainty, unproblematic acceptability become our touchstones.

With reductive reasoning, however, the matter stands on a rather different footing. The touchstone is now not certainty, but something on the order of plausibility, or credibility, or likelihood, or verisimilitude. Here we want to cast our net widely to gather in as much as we can of all those contentions that have something to be said for them. We are not searching for cognitive solid citizens alone, but are involved in gathering in as many plausible prospects as we can get hold of. Our view of acceptability changes from acceptable as certain to acceptable as a credible prospect—from outright endorsement to serious entertainment.

Deductivist epistemology is expansive. It begins with premises as categorical commitments and looks to their logical or probable consequences. By contrast, coherentist epistemology is reductive. It begins with inconsistent data and looks to take more harmonious reduction that is available on the basis of plausibility considerations. The coherence analysis begins with inconsistent data and then in as-

sessing their cognitive merit endeavors to break the chain of inconsistency at its plausibilistically weakest link. And seen in this light,
the coherence theory of truth effectively constitutes the aporetic approach to rational inquiry.[12]

▶3◀

Counterfactual Conditionals

Imaginative impossibilities do not figure only in discourse but have even come to play an increasingly prominent part in modern art. But of course they are most prominent in discursive speculation and especially in the context of speculative suppositions where they have long played a prominent role—especially in matters of imaginative if-then hypothesizing.

Surely things might have been very different. Caesar might not have crossed the Rubicon. Napoleon might never have left Elba. Surely we can reason sensibly from such straightforward contrary-to-fact assumptions so as to obtain instructive information about the consequences and the ramifications of such unrealized possibilities. There can be little question that we can generally say something about "what would happen if" in such matters. Counterfactual conditionals of this sort have been a mainstay of speculative thinking for a long time. The Greek historian Herodotus (b. ca. 480 B.C.) reasoned as follows: "If the Elesian winds were the cause of the Nile's annual flooding, then other rivers would be affected in the same way (which they are not)."[1] What we have here is a *counterfactual conditional*: an answer to a question that asks what would transpire if, where this antecedent is false—or judged to be so.[2]

Just as explanations answer "why" questions, counterfactual conditionals offer responses to "what if" questions. And, clearly, there are both falsifying and truthifying counterfactuals, respectively coordinated with the questions:

If *p* (which is true) were false, then what?

If *p* (which is false) were true, then what?

Answering such falsifying and truthifying questions is the very reason for being of counterfactual conditionals. Such conditionals have been a mainstay of speculative thinking for a long time. And they arise over a wide range of subject matters, including the following:

1. Thought-experimentation in tracing through the consequences of a disbelieved proposition (this occurs both in common life and in technical contexts)

2. Explanation of how things work in general—even under conditionals not actually realized

3. The didactic use of hypotheses in learning situations

4. Contingency planning (in everyday life)

5. Games and make-believe of all kinds

6. Framing expressions of regret or encouragement

7. *Reductio ad absurdum* reasoning and especially *per impossible* proof (in logic and in mathematics)

The psychology of counterfactual thinking is a large and fertile field for psychological investigation.[3] However, our present concern is with the logico-conceptual aspect of the matter—that is, with the rationale of correct thought about these counterfactuals rather than the empirical question of how people generally do think about them.

Counterfactual issues accordingly play a prominent part in both scientific and in common-life thinking, and arise over an enormously wide spectrum of applications, ranging from the most serious to the most frivolous of contexts. And there are many reasons why counterfactuals are important. For one, we can hardly claim that some account satisfactorily explains the occurrence of an event if we cannot establish counterfactually that were the account different that occurrence would not have happened. Only where counterfactuals are satisfactorily at our disposal can we lay claim to an adequate explanatory understanding of the actual facts, and since the 1990s philosophers have given much attention to the topic.[4]

Counterfactual conditionals pivot on suppositions seen as false—along the lines of "If Napoleon had stayed on Elba, the battle of Waterloo would never have been fought." Such counterfactuals *purport to elicit a consequence from an antecedent that is a belief-contradicting supposition, one that it conflicts with the totality of what we take ourselves to know.*[5] Such conditionals have antecedents that involve *conflicts* with our beliefs and not just mere *supplementations* to them. The result is a self-contradictory chaos, and distinctive new instrumentalities need to be provided to restore order.

Supposition is, of course, a commonplace device that functions via such familiar locutions as "suppose," "assume," "what if," "let it be that," "consider the hypothesis that," and the like. This sort of thing is closely connected with our topic since it affords the only other cognitive pathway to the domain of nonexistent possibility. Propositions in general—suppositions included—can be classed in three groups:

1. The factual: those we take to be true: ("Suppose that someone is presently walking on the Champs Élisées")

2. The undecided: those we neither accept nor reject: cognitively indeterminate theses considered neither definitely true nor definitely false ("Suppose that someone checks *War and Peace* out of the town library today")

3. The counterfactual: those we take to be false ("Suppose that all New Yorkers leave town today")

As regards the last category, we can, of course, say a great deal about nonactual states of affairs. But we can only do so when we proceed in the suppositional mode: "If the Easter Bunny existed, it would bring eggs to children on Easter Sunday morning."

A *counterfactual* conditional is accordingly an antecedent that is belief contravening in contradicting accepted beliefs and must thereby be seen as false, as per:

If Paris were in Paraguay, then it would not be in Europe.

The counterfactuality of a conditional is a matter of the status of its antecedent, not its conclusion. Thus consider the counterfactual: "Even if Japan had not bombed Pearl Harbor on December 7, 1941, the United States would (still) have declared war on Japan that month." To make a go of this counterfactual one would depend on something like the following set of beliefs:

1. Japan attacked the Dutch and British possessions in the Far East in December 1941.

2. Japan's attacking Britain's and Holland's Far Eastern colonies in 1941 suffices to provide the United States with a *casus belli*.

Against this background, the Pearl Harbor attack would be seen as a matter of causal overkill in relation to the American declaration of war. And the truth status of the conclusion thus becomes irrelevant to the counterfactuality of the conditional.

It is common among logicians and language theorists nowadays to regard counterfactual suppositions as engendering an involvement with merely possible worlds. The basic idea is that, even though in actuality (in "the real world") the antecedent of the conditional is false, in all duly relevant possible worlds in which the antecedent obtains, the consequent will also hold. Relationships among possible worlds are thus taken to provide the key to the interpretation of counterfactual conditionals.

In fact, however, such a position is very questionable. For what makes a counterfactual conditional acceptable is—as we shall see—simply a suitable understanding of conditions in *this* world, and not a hypothetical leap to some alternative reality.

The task of the present deliberations is accordingly to show how an adequate theory of counterfactuals is able to dispense altogether with the machinery of possible worlds. Exactly because the specification of possible worlds encounters grave difficulties, it becomes worthwhile to explore the prospects of a very different approach to the analysis of counterfactuals.[6] The crux of the presently contemplated approach to their construction lies in seeing counterfactuals as apories generated by suppositions. For any "counterfactual conditional" on the lines of "If Napoleon had stayed on Elba, the battle of Waterloo would never have been fought" is, in effect, *a conditional that elicits a consequence from an antecedent that is a belief-contravening supposition*—one which, by conflicting with the rest of what we take ourselves to know, plays us into a situation of aporetic inconsistency.[7]

> *Belief-Contravening Suppositions Engender Apories*
>   *that Require Resolution*

Hypothetical alterations in the manifold of fact lead us to embark on a process that potentially has no end. Thus suppose that we make only a very small alteration in the descriptive composition of the real, say by adding one pebble to the river bank. But which pebble? Where are we to get it and what are we to put in its place? And where are we to put the air or the water that this new pebble displaces? And when we put that material in a new spot, just how are we to make room for it? And how are we to make room for the so-displaced material? Moreover, the region within six inches of the new pebble used to hold N pebbles now holds $N + 1$. Of which region are we to say holds

$N - 1$. If it is that region yonder, then how did the pebble get here from there? By a miraculous instantaneous transport? By a little boy picking it up and throwing it? But then which little boy? And how did he get there? And if he threw it, then what happened to the air that his throw displaced which would otherwise have gone undisturbed? Here problems arise without end. Every hypothetical change in the physical makeup of the real sets in motion a vast cascade of physical changes either in the physical constitution of the real or in the laws of nature at large. For what about the structure of the envisioning electromagnetic, thermal, and gravitational fields? Just how are these to be preserved, given the removal and/or shift of the pebbles? How is matter to be readjusted to preserve consistency here? Or are we to do so by changing the fundamental laws of physics?

If overall coherence is to be achieved in the wake of a belief-contradicting supposition, it requires various deletions from the body of preexisting belief.[8] For in the wider context of all the prevailing beliefs, counterfactual hypotheses are always paradoxical because *every belief-contradicting hypothesis poses conflicts with other available beliefs—conflicts that will require further adjudication.* The reality of it is that the logico-conceptual interlinkage of our beliefs is such that belief-contradictory suppositions always function within a wider setting of accepted beliefs $p_1, p_2, \ldots, p_n$ of such a sort that when one of them, for simplicity say p_1, must be abandoned owing to a hypothetical endorsement of its negation, nevertheless the resulting group $\sim p_1$, $p_2, \ldots, p_n$ still remains collectively inconsistent.

The systemic integrity of fact indicates that we cannot make hypothetical modifications in the makeup of the real without thereby destabilizing everything and raising an unending series of questions. And not only *redistributions* raise problems; mere *erasures*, mere cancellations do so as well because, reality being as is, they require redistributions to follow in their wake. If by hypothesis we zap a book on the shelf out of existence, then what is it that supports the others? And at what stage of its production did it first disappear? And if it just vanished a moment ago, then what of the law of the conservation of matter? And from whence did the material come that is now in that book-denuded space? Once more we embark upon a complex and baffling journey.

In order to avert such difficulties, there must be some further guidance as to which antecedent belief should be retained and which abandoned when a counterfactual hypothesis is projected. Accordingly, R. M. Chisholm added the proviso that only some *suitable* beliefs are to be retained with others, deemed unsuitable, and thereby abandoned. However, he never managed to provide any satisfactory account for implementing this condition of suitability.[9] And so, if a workable derivability theory of counterfactuals is to be obtained, then special measures will have to be derived to remedy this deficiency by specifying just which beliefs are to be available for the deductive work at issue.

Unfortunately, however, a consistency-restoring belief-abandonment can invariably be accomplished in various different ways.

Thus suppose that tigers were canines. Of course, this hypothesis arises in a context in which we, of course, know each of the following:

1. Tigers are felines.
2. Tigers are not canines.
3. No felines are canines.

The assumption at hand explicitly amounts to Not-2. But what of those other two theses? Are we to alter the boundaries of the classification "felines" (and so drop 1 as well), or to keep these boundaries the same and so countenance tigers as somehow combination canines/felines (thus dropping 3)? Obviously we must, in the interests of mere self-consistency, adopt one or the other of these procedures if logical paradox is to be avoided. And there are always conflicting alternatives in such cases. And the assumption itself gives us no directions for effecting the choice that arises here. This problematic situation portends problems for the analysis of counterfactuals. For the reality of it is that no purely formal logical resources will resolve the issue of such discrepant counterfactuals.

Accordingly, some logical-external, "material" or substantive mechanisms have to be introduced. Whenever an inconsistent group of theses confronts us—say $p \lor r$ and $\sim p$ and $\sim r$—the call that logic can tell us is that at least one of them must be abandoned. But the question of which way to go is something that considerations of logic and abstract theory cannot provide. It emerges that counterfactual reasoning, like inductive reasoning, is ultimately a primarily functional project whose management requires pragmatic resources.[10] And at this point we shall need to turn from theoretical logic to substantive considerations of communicative practice.[11] Let us consider more closely how this is to be implemented.

Logic as such does not tell us what propositions are true but only what inferences are valid—and thereby what we have to accept as true *if* certain statements (the premises) are true. Analogously, counterfactuals will emerge as correct (tenable as truths), only *if* suitable substantive considerations are introduced upon the stage of deliberation.

The difficulty is that when a belief-contradicting hypothesis is projected, at least some of the environing beliefs must always be abandoned in the wake of the hypothetical assumption. And this elimination can invariably be accomplished in various different ways. For instance, contrast the "natural" counterfactual:

> If wood conducted electricity, then this stick would conduct electricity (since it is made of wood).

with the "unnatural" counterfactual:

> If wood conducted electricity, then this stick would not be made of wood (since it does not conduct electricity).

As this example indicates, once we introduce that belief-contravening hypothesis different possibilities for readjustment arise. And since *alternative* outcomes are always possible in such cases, a logical analysis of the situation will not of itself be sufficient to eliminate the basic indeterminacy inherent in counterfactual situations.

In order to avert such difficulties there must be some further guidance as to which antecedent belief should be retained and which abandoned. Accordingly, R. M. Chisholm added the proviso that only some *suitable* beliefs are to be retained. However, he never managed to indicate any satisfactory means for implementing this condition of suitability.[12] And so, if a workable derivability theory of counterfactuals is to be obtained, then it is needful to remedy this deficiency by making it possible to determine just which beliefs are to be available for the deductive work at issue.

Consider such a typical counterfactual conditional as "If wishes were horses, then beggars would ride." It is clear that this contention occurs in the setting of an overall context where the following situation obtains in point of propositional acceptance:

ACCEPTED PROPOSITIONS:

1. Beggars lack the funds to realize their wish for horses. [Fact about beggars.]

2. People who have a useful resource at their disposal (e.g., those who have horses) will generally make use of it (i.e., ride those horses) on appropriate occasions. [General fact about a human modus operandi.]

3. Beggars do not (generally) ride horses. [Fact about beggars.]

COUNTERFACTUAL SUPPOSITION:

Suppose Not-1; that is, suppose that beggars *could* realize their wish for horses.

Note that an apory arises here through inconsistency within the group as a whole. How are we to come to terms with this? Clearly, that stipulated supposition means that we must automatically abandon accepted proposition 1 if consistency is to be maintained. But this is not enough. For given Not-1, 2 entails that beggars would generally ride, and this contradicts 3. Having dropped 1, we must thus also drop either 2 or 3, since the propositional commitments of the set {Not-1, 2, 3} still constitute an inconsistent group. Two alternatives accordingly lie before us as regards acceptance/rejection: 2/1, 3 or 3/1, 2. Here 1 must be abandoned in any case, thanks to the supposition at issue. And either 2 must yield to 3 or the other way around.

Now abstract logic alone, without any substantive supplementation, can carry us no further than the indecisive upshot: If Not-1, then either Not-2 or Not-3. But considerations of plausibility regarding precedence and priority among propositions that conflict straightaway validates the counterfactual contention at issue. For observe that when, as is only reasonable in these merely hypothetical situations, we adopt the substantive policy of *making facts of lesser generality give way to facts of greater lawful generality*, this means that we would abandon thesis 3 in favor of 2, thereby arriving at the first option (2/1, 3), so as to validate the counterfactual: "If beggars could realize their wish for horses, then beggars would (generally) ride."

The principle of generality precedence is once again illustrated by the counterfactual "If he had been born in 1999, then Julius Caesar would be an infant now (2000)." This arises in the following context:

ACCEPTED PROPOSITIONS:

1. Julius Caesar was born in 100 B.C.

2. Julius Caesar is now (2000) long dead, having died at the age of fifty-six in 44 B.C.

3. Julius Caesar was not born in 1999 A.D.

4. Anyone born in 1999 A.D. will be an infant now (2000).

ASSUMPTION:

Not-3; that is, Julius Caesar was born in 1999 A.D.

Now accepting the assumption—as one must—we note that it explicitly instructs us to dismiss 1 and 3. But we are still driven to make a choice between 2 and 4. Two alternatives thus stand before us as regards acceptance/rejection: 4/1, 2, 3 or 2/1, 3, 4. And at this stage, generality precedence constrains us to jettison 2, thus retaining 4 and Not-3. The conclusion of our counterfactual at once follows.

Again, consider the counterfactual: "If this rubber band were made of copper, then it would conduct electricity." Here we have the following situation:

ACCEPTED PROPOSITIONS:

1 This band is made (i.e., *predominantly* made) of rubber.

2. This band is not made of copper.

3. This band does not conduct electricity.

4. Objects made of rubber do not conduct electricity.

5. Objects made of copper do conduct electricity.

ASSUMPTION:

Not-2; that is, this band is made of copper.

Note that even with accepted proposition 2 deleted from the givens 1–5, the result of adding Not-2 still leaves us with an inconsistent set of propositions. Given this state of affairs, two consistency-restoring alternatives stand before us as regards acceptance/rejection: 3, 4/1, 2, 5 or 4, 5/1, 2, 3. In these circumstances, 1 and 2 will have to be rejected come what may, and 4 is an innocent bystander that can be retained come what may. The only residual issue is whether to make 3 give way to 5 or the other way round. Here, again, if in these purely hypothetical situations we adopt the aforementioned policy of having facts of greater generality prevail, then we would arrive at the second option (4, 5/1, 2, 3) and thereby validate that initial counterfactual: "If the rubber band were copper, it would conduct electricity." Such examples convey larger lessons.

▶ Weakest-Link Determination and the Centrality of Precedence (Right of Way)

Counterfactuals are bound to engender perplexity because *all reality-modifying assumptions are contextually ambiguous*. For once we assume that Not-*p* in a context where *p* is already in place, we embark on an endless succession of yet-unresolved choices. For suppose we accept *p*. Then for any arbitrary *q* for which we accept Not-*q* we are also committed to *p* ∨ *q*. We thus (by hypothesis) stand committed to:

p

$p \lor q$

Not-q

But now when *p* is replaced by Not-*p* so that the first thesis is negated, we shall have to reject at least one of the other two. But we have no purely logical guidance as to which way to go. The situation is totally ambiguous in this regard, and logic as such can offer us no succor. When an inconsistency arises, all that logic can do is to insist that consistency must be restored. It will not tell us *how* to do this. This requires some altogether extralogical resource along lines exemplified by the generality-priority principle deployed earlier. The pivotal idea is that of brevity, the chain of inconsistency at its weakest link (Weakest Link Principle).

For in the context of prevailing beliefs, *counterfactual hypotheses are always paradoxical*.[13] For each of our beliefs is encased within a family of others in such a way that the introduction of a belief-countervailing assumption introduces logical inconsistencies. Now the resolution of these inconsistencies can in theory always be accomplished in a variety of different ways, since in such conflicts there are always alternative ways of making some of the conflict-engendering beliefs give way to others. To decide the matter definitely and remove the ambiguity at issue, we require additional, hypothesis-transcending information—specifically, a mechanism of precedence and priority to enable us to choose among the alternatives that confront us. We need to find the weakest link. And generality or scope is the key factor here.

Confronted with an inconsistent set of otherwise plausible propositions in any domain of inquiry, it is only rational to seek to restore consistency. Something has to give way in the interests of coherence. And the standard approach here is to break the chain of inconsistency at its weakest link(s).

However, this business of weakest-link determination functions rather differently in different areas of inquiry in alignment with the variation of the purposive nature of the context of thought at issue. For of course different cognitive enterprises will have aims and objectives in view. To illustrate this situation consider the following example, due in its essentials to Nelson Goodman:[14]

ACCEPTED PROPOSITIONS:

1. New York City is located in New York State.
2. New York State is disjoint from Georgia.
3. New York City is not located in Georgia.

ASSUMPTION:

Not-3; that is, New York City is located in Georgia.

Two alternatives now stand before us as regards acceptance/rejection: 1/2, 3 or 2/1, 3.

Here 3 must of course be rejected come what may. But we then have a choice between 1 and 2—that is, between changing the location of New York City or changing the location of certain entire states. The question is, which gets the priority, 1 or 2? Depending on which alternative is adopted, we would validate one of the following counterfactuals:

If New York City were in Georgia, then New York City would not be located in New York State.

If New York City were in Georgia, then Georgia would overlap with New York State.

It is clear, however, that the first alternative qualifies as the more natural of the two, seeing that in the effort to protect generality, it is clearly less drastic to relocate cities than to relocate entire states. Here, as elsewhere, we would want to make more generally disruptive alternatives give way to those that are less so.

For the sake of a further illustration, consider the following example due to David Lewis.[15] The case at issue is by stipulation one where we are taken to know the following:

1. J. F. Kennedy was assassinated.

2. J. H. Oswald assassinated Kennedy.

3. No one other than Oswald assassinated Kennedy.

Suppose now that we are instructed to suppose Not-2, and to assume the Kennedy was not killed by Oswald. Then we clearly cannot retain both 1 and 3, since in the presence of Not-2, 3 entails that no one assassinated Kennedy, which contradicts 1. Either 1 or 3 must go—one must be subordinated to the other. In such a case, the very way in which a counterfactual is formulated can adequately instruct us as to the appropriate resolutions:

A. If Oswald did not assassinate Kennedy, then someone else did. [Subordinates 3 to 1.]

B. If Oswald had not assassinated Kennedy, then Kennedy would not have been assassinated at all. [Subordinates 1 to 3.]

However, if we were to supplement our beliefs 1–3 with a conspiracy theory by way of adopting

4. Kennedy was the victim of a successful assassination conspiracy.

then we would also arrive at

C. If Oswald had not assassinated Kennedy, then someone else would have. [Subordinates 3 to 4.]

Comparing C with A shows that the very way in which these conditionals are formulated often informs us about (and corresponds to) the sorts of subordination relationships that are at work among those "factual" items that we accept as fundamental within the information-context of the counterfactual at issue.

As all such examples indicate, the resolution of apories arising in the wake of counterfactual hypotheses pivots on principles of precedence—on the availability of principles to determine the allocation of the right-of-way in cases of propositional conflict, thereby enabling the chain of inconsistency to be broken. The validation of counterfactuals lies in the comparative prioritization of the relevant beliefs, be it through explicit instructions or tacit guiding principles.

The salient point is that to deal effectively with counterfactual conditionals we must be in a position to distinguish, within the group of logically eligible alternatives, between more and less "natural" ways of reconciling a belief-contravening hypothesis with the entire set of residual beliefs that continue to be collectively inconsistent with it. And only considerations of substantive priority—be they explicitly stated or merely tacit—can avert immobilization at this point. They enable us both to validate counterfactual conditionals and to explain how it is that some counterfactuals are natural and acceptable and others unnatural and unacceptable. For in all such conflict situations we require a functional analogue of a traffic director at a road intersection to determine who is to have the right of way, indicating which statements are to give way to the others in cases of conflict.

It is instructive in this regard to consider the following Bizet-Verdi example, due to W. V. Quine.[16] Are we to have:

"If Bizet and Verdi were fellow countrymen, then Bizet would be Italian."

or

"If Bizet and Verdi were fellow countrymen, then Verdi would be French."

Here two salient facts lie before us:

1. Bizet was a Frenchman.

2. Verdi was an Italian

These contentions are altogether on par with one another in point of generality, so that the usual considerations of priority are of no avail here. However, an indication of priority here may well be produced by a more elaborate formulation of the question we propose to address. There are three major possibilities here:

A. If Bizet were a countryman of Verdi's, what nationality would they be?

B. If Verdi were a countryman of Bizet's, what nationality would they be?

C. If Bizet and Verdi were fellow countrymen, what nationality would they be?

With the first wording of the question—namely, A—we are, in effect, instructed to prioritize 2 over 1. With wording B, the reverse is the case and 2 gains the priority over 1. But the third wording—namely, C—deliberately avoids priority guidance, and for that very reason permits no definite conclusion. In this case all that we can say with confidence is that:

If Bizet and Verdi were fellow countrymen, then either both would be French or both would be Italian.

In the absence of any guidance with respect to precedence and priority, this takes us no further than an indefinite disjunction of alternatives. Since there is no *weakest* link, this indecisively feeble counterfactual is the best that we can now manage.[17]

▸ *The Question of Rationale*

It is striking that the standard presumption at issue with specificity prioritization is in fact inverted and the reverse procedure, a generality prioritization, obtains when we turn from factual to counterfactual contexts. Thus consider the counterfactual conditional:

If he had been born in 1999, then Julius Caesar would not have died in 44 B.C. but would be a mere infant in 2000.

This arises in the context of the following issue-salient beliefs:

1. Julius Caesar was born in 100 B.C.

2. Julius Caesar is long dead, having died at the age of fifty-six in 44 B.C.

3. Julius Caesar was not born in 1999 A.D.

4. Anyone born in 1999 A.D. will only be an infant by 2000.

5. People cannot die before they are born.

And let us now introduce the supposition of Not-3 via the following:

ASSUMPTION:

Suppose Not-3; that is, Julius Caesar was born in 1999 A.D.

In the face of this assumption we must, of course, follow its explicit instruction to dismiss 1 and 3. However, 4 is safe, inherent in the very definition of infancy. Even with these readjustments, though, inconsistency remains and confronts us with two distinct acceptance/rejection alternatives: 2, 4/1, 3, 5 or 4, 5/1, 2, 3. In effect we are constrained to a choice between the specific 2, on the one hand, and the general 5, on the other. At this point, however, the natural resolution afforded by the now operative Principle of Fundamentality Precedence has us prioritize the more general and instance-encompassing 5 over the case-specific 2, effectively eliminating that first alternative. Given Not-1, the conclusion of the initial counterfactual then at once follows from 4 and 5.

As this example illustrates, *deliberating from fact-contradicting assumptions we operate with fundamentality precedence*. And this betokens a larger lesson: In determining which beliefs should give way in the face of counterfactual assumptions, systemic fundamentality and informativeness should be our guide. Accordingly, in counterfactual contexts, generalities take precedence over specificities. In factual contexts we prioritize evidentiation; here, in cases of conflict, the more strongly evidentiated proposition wins out. But in counterfactual contexts we proceed differently. Here it is fundamentality rather than evidentiation that matters.

This crucial difference between factual and counterfactual situations in relation to evidentiation can be illustrated as follows. Consider the following situation.

BELIEFS:

1. John is married to Mary. [Strongly evidentiated belief.]

2. John is married to Jane. [Weakly evidentiated belief.]

3. John is a bigamist. [Firm belief.]

Now in this belief situation, let us suppose that in place of 3 we had its negative:

Not-3: John is not a bigamist.

We would then arrive at the factual conditional

Since John is not a bigamist, then (almost certainly) he did not marry Jane. If Not-3, then Not-2.

In such factual cases, the chain of inconsistency has its weak link at the evidentially weakest point.

However, in the counterfactual (purely speculative) cases, we do not and should not reason in this way. Here we would *not* conclude the following:

If John were not a bigamist, then he would (very likely) not have married Jane.

All we can arrive at is

If John were not a bigamist, then he would certainly not have married both Mary and Jane.

In these circumstances, the guidance of general principles carries us no further than this indefinite result.

In the context of counterfactuality, rational procedure is now a matter of keeping our systemic grip on the manifold of relevant information as best we can. Once we enter the realm of fact-contravening hypotheses, those general theses and themes that we subordinate to specifics in factual matters now become our life preservers. We cling to them for dear life, as it were, and do all that is necessary to keep them in place. Salvage as much information about the actual state of things as you possibly can. Accordingly, specifics and particularities will understandably yield way to generalizations and abstractions. And so in determining which beliefs are to give way in the face of counterfactual assumptions, we let systemic fundamentality and informativeness be our guide. Keeping our systemic grip on the manifold of relevant information is the crux, and speaks clearly for generality precedence. Lawfulness (in the sense of natural law) and generality of range are pivotal features in the treatment of counterfactuals.[18] The overall lesson then is clear: When a clash among seemingly acceptable propositions occurs in *factual* contexts, considerations of evidential plausibility lead us to adopt the stance of specificity preference. But in counterfactual contexts where the economics of information management is paramount, our deliberations must pivot the generality preference at issue with systemic cogency.

To be sure, in the case of a counterfactual supposition that is itself particular, we may have to make a generalization give way to it. This arises standardly in the case of thought experiments that contemplate outcomes that may defeat generalizations. Thus consider the following counterfactual relating to the generalization (g) that heavy objects (like rocks) fall to earth when released:

> If this heavy rock had not fallen to earth when it was released at altitude yesterday, then g would be false.

Here we have the following beliefs regarding the facts of the situation:

1. That heavy rock was released at altitude yesterday. [Fact.]
2. That rock then fell to earth. [Fact.]

3. Heavy objects (like rocks) fall to earth when released at
   altitude (g). [Law.]

When now instructed to assume Not-2, the resulting inconsistency
forces a choice between abandoning the specific (1) and the general
(3). With generality precedence at work, we would be constrained to
retain 3. But that of course is not how things work in such a thought
experiment. For now the particular thesis at issue—namely, 1—is
here immunized against rejection by the circumstance of its constituting part of the very hypothesis at issue. All in all, then, the
aporetic method affords a natural and effective means for reasoning
in the context of counterfactual speculation.

4

Variant Analyses of Counterfactuals and Problems of Probability

▶*Alternative Approaches to Counterfactual Analysis:*
Ramsey's Change-Minimization Test

There exist several influential approaches to the analysis of counterfactuals that are very different from the aporetic strategy of the preceding chapters. The earliest of these was first proposed in the 1920s by the English philosopher-logician Frank P. Ramsey. It was effectively encapsulated in the following thesis:

> A conditional "If *p*, then *q*" is acceptable in the context of a body of belief if accepting *q* is required by the result of making the minimal changes in the body of beliefs required to accommodate *p*.[1]

This minimal belief-revision standard for counterfactual conditionals is perhaps less of a specific tactic for handling them than a general strategy aptly called "the Ramsey test" by William Harper.[2] It is in some ways a forerunner of our present approach, since it too proceeds on a doxastic and thus epistemic basis. However, it is also substantially different—as will soon become evident.

Ramsey's strategy has been formulated by Robert Stalnaker as follows:

> This is how to evaluate a [counterfactual] conditional. First, add the antecedent hypothetically to your stock of beliefs; second, make whatever adjustments are [minimally] required to maintain consistency (without modifying the hypothetical belief in the antecedent); finally consider whether or not the consequent is [then entailed as] true.[3]

However, the unfortunate fact of it is that the simple-sounding process of belief revision comes to logical shipwreck on the systemic integrity of fact. Thus suppose I believe p. I then have little choice but to include among my beliefs both p-or-q and p-or-not-q, where q is any arbitrary proposition whatsoever. Let us now consider a conditional of the format

If not-p, then . . .

There are then two different alternative minimal readjustments (viz., dropping $p \lor q$ and dropping $p \lor \sim q$), and they yield squarely conflicting conditionals:

If $\sim p$, then q

If $\sim p$, then not-q

So when supposing $\sim p$, the minimal revision process appears to commit us to both q and not-q (for *arbitrary* q). This circumstance raises major difficulties for Ramsey's approach. For the problem is that there simply is no such thing as a uniquely acceptable minimal revision. Certainly, Ramsey himself did not offer much guidance as to how that minimally revised belief-set B is to be formed; he left working out the idea of a minimalistic revision as an exercise for the reader. But this is a problem that faces substantial obstacles:

Variant Analyses of Counterfactuals

1. Minimality requires a quantitative comparison in part of size. But what is to make one revision greater or lesser than another given the unending potential for the internal complexity of what is involved?

2. Minimality becomes impracticable in slippery-slope situations where additional steps toward enhanced differentiation are always possible.

3. Can the idea of a "minimal assumption-accommodating revision" of a belief set be implemented at all? Is a well-defined concept at issue here? Is minimality something we can actually realize in the situation of counterfactual reasoning?

As regards point 1, let it be there are three beagles in the yard and I stipulate "Assume there are two beagles." How are our change-minimizing deliberations to proceed here? Are we to annihilate one beagle? (And which one?) Or should we retain that "There are three dogs in the yard" and replace that missing beagle with another dog? (And if so, one of what species?) Or should one contract the yard a bit and thus eliminate one beagle from it? The mind boggles.

As regards point 2, consider a supposition like "Suppose the storm had lasted longer than it had." How are we to think of an alternative that differs minimally: in days, in hours, in minutes, in seconds, in milliseconds, etc.? The minimizing of change is clearly impracticable.

Finally, as regards point 3, let it be that Bob weighs 182 pounds. So does Tom. They balance on the teeter-totter. But we will now have the (true) counterfactual:

If Bob's weight differed from Tom's, then one of them would rise to the top on the teeter-totter.

Yet here, with respect to this difference in weight, there simply is no belief system that both realizes the antecedent and differs minimally from the actual situation. In other words, there simply is no *minimal* revision here in the overall family of relevant belief.

Yet another objection to Ramsey's minimal belief revision standard is that it leads to various counterintuitive results.[4] Thus consider:

If that stuffed owl were still alive, then it would not remain on that shelf tonight but would fly off.

Plausible though this conditional is, it cannot be validated by a minimal belief-revision approach. For in view of its minimality, such a revision would surely keep that revivified owl planted firmly on the shelf—asleep, tethered, walking back and forth in a dazed manner, or some such, all of which yield a world that keeps descriptively closer to the actual than the situation contemplated in the counterfactual's conclusion.

Again, the following example is also instructive in this regard:

BELIEFS:

1. Rover is a lapdog.

2. Rover is a purebred dog.

3. Rover is a prizewinning show dog.

4. All dogs are canines.

5. Rover is a canine.

And now let it be that we are asked to undertake the following supposition:

Not-5; that is, suppose that Rover were not a canine.

We must now abandon not only 5, as per instruction, but also either 4 or all of 1, 2, and 3. On a Ramseyesque minimal-revision we would presumably be led to abandon 4 and retain all the rest (save 5) so as to arrive at:

If Rover were not a canine, then not all dogs would be canines.

This does not seem all that plausible. Observe, for contrast, that the present information-conservation approach with its prioritization of laws requires the retention of 4, thus leading to the counterfactual:

> If Rover were not a canine, then he would not be a purebred, prizewinning lapdog,

which is clearly appropriate in the circumstances.

It is clear that our present approach differs dramatically from Ramsey's. For in contrast to Ramsey's minimal-revision a sensible alternative would not involve the wider manifold of *all* relevant beliefs, but only a look to a small handful of immediately salient items. It thus merely calls for assessing the tenability counterfactuals through deleting some (generally few) members from a manageably small family of issue-relevant beliefs. Moreover, it would not require a foray into the intractable project of change-minimality with respect to the overall manifold of one's beliefs, but merely requires the application of a few rather straightforward prioritization rules. Ramsey's approach relies, in effect, on a process of "imagining" that projects a transformation of one's entire system of belief.[5] However, the present approach involves no comparably arcane complications, but proceeds by applying a modest handful of generally straightforward standards of fundamentality. For on its basis we need never grapple with the entire manifold of our beliefs regarding the world at large; only a few immediately relevant beliefs need ever be brought into it.

Alternative Approaches to Counterfactual Analysis: Lewis's World Proximity Criterion

Another influential approach to counterfactual analysis that has been proposed in recent years is based on a possible-worlds approach inaugurated by Robert Stalnaker. Addressing the question, "How do we decide whether or not to believe a conditional statement," Stalnaker maintained that while Ramsey was on the right track to begin with beliefs, nevertheless:

> The problem is to make the transition from belief conditionals to truth conditionals . . . [and here] the concept of a *pos-*

sible world is just what we need to make the transition, since a possible world is the ontological analogue of a stock hypothetical belief. [And so] the following is a final approximation to the account I shall propose: Consider a possible world in which *A* is true and which otherwise differs minimally from that actual world. "If *A* then *B*" is true (false) just as case *B* is true (false) in that possible world.[6]

Stalnaker's proposal was subsequently extended and developed via what might be called the World-Proximity Criterion of David Lewis. For in a series of publications of the 1970s, Lewis proposed a semantical, possible-worlds approach to counterfactuals in which their tenability is determined in terms of "proximity" relations among possible worlds.[7] And at least in Lewis's earlier papers proximity is to be determined on the basis of descriptive similarity, though in later papers lawfulness comes to play a more prominent role.

Let us suppose that "They tell me you will *depart* tomorrow." And now consider the question: Suppose that that italicized word were not "depart," what would it then be? Clearly in addressing this question we would follow the Lewis principle and seek an alternative that is as close to the actualities as possible—thus opting for an alternative along the lines of *leave* or *go*. But this is a rather special sort of situation. It would make little sense to address the question "What if France had not decided to give the Statue of Liberty to the U.S.A.?" with the response "Then France would have given some other vast bronze statue by Bartholdi instead," even though this would keep the resulting world maximality similar to the actual one. Only in very special sorts of cases is the Stalnaker-Lewis similarity approach to counterfactuality in order.

There is a substantial difference between Stalnaker's and Lewis's treatment of counterfactuals and that of the presently articulated approach. For theirs is a metaphysical theory based on the invocation of possible worlds, while the present theory is epistemic and thus not encumbered with the metaphysical baggage of merely possible worlds and merely possible objects. Such possibilia, whatever their ontology and their problems, are something very different from sets of beliefs, which can, after all, be finite in scope and incomplete, and indeed sometimes even inconsistent.[8]

However, it is clearly damaging to the Stalnaker-Lewis descriptive similarity approach that we would presumably want to say, "If John F. Kennedy had not been assassinated on November 22, 1963, then he (and not Lyndon Johnson) would have delivered the State of the Union message in January of 1964." And yet, clearly, a world in which JFK was assassinated on the day preceding or following the Dallas shooting—and thus unable to give that address—looks to be one descriptively far closer, and thus more similar, to the actual world.

Then, too, a world in which there had been one fewer casualty in the Battle of the Bulge is in its way more similar to the actualities of our world than one in which there had been yet more. But the conditional, "If there had been fewer causalities in the Battle of the Bulge then there actually were, there would have been just one fewer of them," does not look all that plausible.

Additionally, the world-similarity approach also encounters other, more substantial problems. To begin with, there are all of the *practical* difficulties of applying this idea; for example, there is the question of where alternative possible worlds are to come from and how we are to get there from here.[9] But even waiving this problem, how is the idea of world-similarity (or "proximity") to be implemented? after all, given that "similarity" splits apart into an endless multiplicity of respects—even as people can be similar in appearance and dissimilar in personality, or the reverse. Given the proliferation of respects, how can the idea of absolute, across-the-board similarity possibly be implemented? And even if respects are taken into account, how could this be done by some stably context-transcendent weighting? Moreover, which mode of similarity is to prevail: the phenomenologically descriptive or the structural? How is one to cope with *different* modes of resemblance?

One may be tempted to respond by maintaining that it is qualitative description rather than quantitative structure that matters for world similarity. But before taking this line, consider the case of three maps of Europe: one actual and two altered alternatives. In one alternative only the colors of the countries are changed. In the other, the colors are kept the same but the shapes (i.e., country boundaries) are slightly modified. Which of these changelings is closer to the original map? Here it would clearly be structural rather than phenomenologically descriptive similarity that matters. As such examples indicate, it would be inappropriate to operate with the idea of similarity in any sort of standardized way.

The prime difficulty is that whenever there is a plurality of different respects there is no single coherent way of moving from a multiplicity of feature correlative modes of similarity/proximity/changelessness to a single, comprehensive, overall similarity/proximity/changelessness. Is a possible world where horses have horns closer to one where rabbits have pouches? Is a possible world where grass is yellow closer to our world than to a world where figs are white? Is similarity among people in point of dieting preferences more or less important for world distance than similarity in point of pastimes? A multitude of questions of this sort immediately arise from the distance comparison of possible worlds, and there is no practicable way of resolving them.

Consider, for example, the counterfactual:

> If Theodore Roosevelt had appointed Woodrow Wilson ambassador of Germany, then Wilson would have mastered conversational German.

How can we possibly tell which of the worlds in which Theodore Roosevelt appoints Woodrow Wilson ambassador to Germany are "sufficiently close" to ours? And where on earth—or elsewhere—are such worlds to come from?

On the other hand, it is hard to see how Lewis's procedure can avoid endorsing the absurd counterfactual:

> Even if Shakespeare had never been born, *Hamlet* would nevertheless still be performed on the stage today.

After all, a world with *Hamlet* performances (even if based on a mysteriously found script by some unidentifiable poet) would seem to be more similar to our world than one where this drama was among the missing. The long and short of it is that there is only a proliferation of similarities of respect and no such thing as a synoptically comprehensive, everything-considered, all-in similarity.[10]

Just as in personal preference theory there is—by Arrow's paradox—no viable way of extracting a meaningful single overall-preferability index from a variety of preferability respects, so in possible world theory there is no way of extracting a single overall-similarity index from a multiplicity of respect-geared similarities.

Moreover, on a Lewis-style approach we are asked to identify those possible worlds where the antecedent obtains and which are maximally (or sufficiently) similar to this actual world. This done, we are to check that the consequent (always) obtains there. But it is clear that on this approach it is now somewhere between difficult and impossible to know what to make of such seemingly acceptable counterfactuals as:

1. If the big bang had not occurred, then physical matter would not exist.

2. If the physical constants of nature were different, there would be no stable types of material substance.

3. If cosmic evolution had taken a different course, stars would not have evolved.

In such cases we would surely find it somewhere between difficult and impossible to say what antecedent-satisfying possible worlds would be like.

And further sorts of problems arise, even where a single quantitative feature of the world's composition is concerned, in a way that parallels the difficulties afflicting Ramsey's approach. For the Lewis closest-to-reality standard leads to the anomalous result that for every positive ϵ, we would have the counterfactual "If I were over 7 feet tall then I would (still) be under $7 + \epsilon$ feet tall."[11] Such quantitative parameters are bound to create difficulty for a Lewis-style approach.

Analogous difficulties for this approach arise in the context of temporal processes. Thus consider the following situation: at time t I deliberated about whether to do A at $t + t'$ And decide against it. To all plausible appearances we then have the counterfactual:

If I had not decided at t against doing A at $t + t'$, then I would have done A at that time.

But now for any world-scenario in which that antecedent is true (viz., in which I decide at t to do A at $t + t'$) and the consequent also (viz., I do A) there will be a world-possibility *that is more similar to the real-world situation* in which the consequence is false (viz., I do not do A), namely one in which I change my mind soon after t, though before $t + t'$. On this basis the true-in-similar-worlds approach to counterfactuals is in principle precluded from validating counterfactuals of the indicated sort.[12]

For Stalnaker and Lewis, the analysis of counterfactuals unavoidably require a foray into the realm of unactualized possible worlds, scrutinizing those—duly similar to ours—in which the antecedent obtains to see whatever is not the consequence obtains there as well. And in view of Burley's Principle, it is not easy to exaggerate the extent of the difficulty and perplexity that this sort of project involves.

To be sure, as he was eventually confronted with a variety of concrete examples, Lewis, to his credit, recognized such problems and sought to remove them by introducing curative complications. In particular, he grappled with the (ultimately intractable) difficulties of distilling a single overall similarity comparison out of a plurality of similarities in diverse respects. His solution was to have recourse to the idea of combining similarities via an assignment of different weights to different factors, proposing the following "system of weights" to implement the similarity relation for the world-closeness semantics for the truth condition of subjunctive conditionals,[13] the weighting at issue being based on the following:

1. Minimizing large-scale violations of this world's natural laws

2. Maximizing agreement with this world's large-scale facts

3. Minimizing small-scale violations of this world's natural law

4. Maximizing agreement with this world's small-scale facts

While such a move away from phenomenological toward nomic similarity is unquestionably a step in the right direction, it is nowhere near enough to meet the demands of the situation. The multiplicity at issue with similarity of respect is simply going to recur at higher levels. There just is no viable way of implementing that crucial idea of minimization/maximization.

▶*Some Points of Difference*

A closer comparison of the present approach to counterfactual analysis with that of Stalnaker-Lewis is instructive.

Consider drawing a ball from an urn containing one thousand white balls and one black one, and let it be that a white ball is in fact drawn, as is all too probable. And now consider the counterfactual:

> If the drawing had occurred with that number of white and black balls interchanged, a white ball would still have been drawn.

There seems to be no way for a Lewis-style world-similarity approach to avert this result.

However, our present approach averts this outcome. Consider the following salient beliefs:

1. There are 1,001 balls in the urn.

2. 1,000 of these are white, not black.

3. One of them is black, not white.

4. A white ball was drawn.

5. The maximally probable outcome resulted.

We are instructed to replace 2 and 3 respectively with:

2'. 1,000 of them are black, not white.

3'. One of them is white, not black.

Now given that 1 is a fixity, this forces a choice between 4 and 5. And with generality preference ruling in favor of 5 we arrive at:

> If the drawing had occurred with the number of white and black balls interchanged, a black ball would have been drawn.

This is surely the more sensible outcome.

To make the difference of the various approaches still more vivid, let us suppose the following situation to prevail with respect to what we know regarding the content of two boxes, into which Smith has put some coins:

1. Box 1 is empty.

2. Box 2 has two coins in it.

3. There are no pennies in Box 2.

4. Smith did not put a penny into either of the boxes.

But now suppose not-4; that is, assume that Smith had also (additionally) put a penny in one of the boxes.

There are, of course, two possibilities at this point. Smith could have put the penny into Box 1 or into Box 2. Thus two counterfactuals come into our range of contemplation.

A. If Smith had also and additionally put a penny into one of the boxes, this penny would be in Box 1 because Box 2 has no pennies in it. [Here we drop not only 4 but also 1.]

B. If Smith had also and additionally put a penny into one of the boxes, this penny would be in Box 2, since Box 1 is empty. [Here we would drop not only 4, but 2 and 3 as well.]

On Ramsey's account (least change among prevailing beliefs), and also on Lewis's account (determination by the assumption-consistent possible world closest to the actual), the former of these alternatives would presumably prevail, seeing that by leaving 2–4 intact it involves a lesser modification of the status quo defined by the indicated specifications.[14]

Now it might seem that this is also the case with the present account, thanks to crediting 3 with generality precedence. But this appearance is misleading because 3 is no sort of a law of nature but simply a matter of happenstance that has the same footing as 1 and 2. And so we lack adequate priority guidance here. Since in both cases the *overall* plausibility status of what is dropped is the same, we can achieve no more than the pedestrian disjunctive counterfactual:

C. If Smith had put a penny into one of the boxes, then either Box 1 would contain (only) a penny, or Box 2 would have coins in it, only one of which is a penny.

This, on our present account, is the most and the best that can be realized.

The difference between the present approach to counterfactuals and that of Ramsey and Lewis can also be made graphic by considering the situation in which we are confronted by the series:

01010101010101 . . .

To all visible appearances, this series answers to the rule "Alternate 0s and 1s." But now consider the what-if question:

If that first member of the series were 1, what would the second member be?

As with Ramsey's belief conservation and a Stalnaker-Lewis-style world similarity approach, we are now embarked on a problematic course. Granted that by stipulation the first member now has to be a 1. But, of course, there remains the possibility of keeping all the other series members as is, and clearly no other alternative arrangement can possibly be closer to the real-world situation. And so on both approaches we arrive at the following:

> If that first number were a 1, the second number would (still) be a 1.

Given their insistence on descriptive (phenomenological) real-world similarity, both theorists would have to endorse this conditional.

The present approach, however, does not take this line. In prioritizing general rules over descriptive details, we would arrive at:

> If that first member were a 1, the second member would be a 0.

And this is surely the more plausible upshot.

The crux here is that while those alternative approaches are geared to *descriptively phenomenological* approximation to reality, the present law-oriented approach strives for a *nomologically law-oriented* approximation to reality.[15]

To be sure, by the time of his 1979 paper Lewis came to recognize the need for law prioritization. However, this departure from his earlier phenomenological approach still rides roughshod over the difference between conceptually grounded laws of logic and language, on the one hand, and laws of nature, on the other. And it does not reckon with the fact that nature laws themselves can—though applicable always and everywhere—nevertheless be of very different levels of fundamentality. But be this as it may, the gravest objection of the Stalnaker-Lewis possible worlds approach is there is no well-defined and operationally effective way of coming to grips with nonexistent possible worlds. Once we introduce hypothetical modification into the fabric of the real we have no practicable way to effect the totality of necessary readjustments.[16]

A cognate approach to Stalnaker-Lewis is the treatment of counterfactuals developed by my student Igal Kvart and set out in his 1986 book, *A Theory of Counterfactuals*. This approach is inferential in nature—as was that of my 1964 book and Ramsey's own theory before that. However, in analyzing counterfactuals, Kvart proceeds *expansively* by building up a set of "the right" premises, in the manner of Ramsey, whereas I proceed contractively by eliminating the inappropriate premises. These formal differences aside, there is a further fundamental substantive difference between our approaches. As Kvart himself observes, "The distinctive features of the analysis proposed in this book [include] . . . first, a special emphasis . . . put on temporal features."[17] However, this time-orientation of the theory limits it to a rather restrictive range of world-bound conditionals that leaves abstract matters and purely theoretical conditionals entirely out of sight. For example, Kvart's theory could not address, "If the set {1, 5, 9, 13} were to be increased by yet another member, this might well be 17." Nor can it handle such a necessity-contravening counterfactual as "Even if the set of primes had three fewer members than it actually does, it would still have an infinite number of members." Many of the salient weaknesses that characterize such possible world approaches as those of Stalnaker and Lewis continue to restrict the range of application of the cognitive approach espoused by Kvart.

Considerations along the indicated lines show that the three principally variant approaches to counterfactual analysis considered here are in fact predicated on asking quite different questions:

1. Ramsey: What part of the overall belief system will, while also accommodating the hypothesis, include as much as possible from among our actual beliefs? [Belief-retention standard.]

2. Stalnaker-Lewis: What is it that obtains in the possible world arrangement that, while compatible with the hypothesis, comes descriptively closest to (and thus most closely resembles) the arrangements of the real world? [World-proximity standard with proximity construed sometimes descriptively (early Lewis), sometimes nomologically (later Lewis).]

3. Rescher: What is it that obtains when one curtails the contextually salient beliefs in a way that both assures

compatibility with the hypothesis and optimizes the retention of pre-hypothesis information in light of the apposite prioritization-standards (viz., considerations of fundamentability)? [Information-conservation standard.]

The specific implementation of these approaches shows that there are different questions that, as our examples show, have different answers and lead to different results in different cases—results which differ decidedly in their acceptability.

To summarize: The current scene affords three prime alternatives for counterfactual analysis: Ramsey's minimal revision approach, Lewis's world-similarity maximization approach, and the present book's optimal resystemization approach based on a systematic reconstruction of our belief system using the principles of *saliency* (issue-significance) and *prioritization* (informativeness-precedence). And the claims to superiority of that third alternative reside in two principal considerations:

1. Unlike the alternatives, it does not make virtually unrealizable demands (surveying possible worlds, recasting entire belief systems) but only requires scrutinizing a handful of immediately relevant beliefs.

2. As many concrete examples show, it more adequately accommodates the presystematic acceptability and inductive appropriateness of counterfactual inferences.

▶ The Dispensability of Nonexistent Possible Worlds

Contemporary philosophers incline almost without exception to the view that alternative possibilities require alternative worlds. Thus consider "If there were no cats in the world, dogs would be even more popular as pets than they now are." Regarding this counterfactual, these theorists would maintain that we cannot really make sense of it without contemplating possible worlds, alternative to ours, from which cats are missing." But the presently contemplated approach to counterfactuals puts this view into a very dubious light. Consider the following situation:

ACCEPTED PROPOSITIONS:

1. Some people who do not own dogs would get one if cats were not available.
2. Cats are available.
3. There are n dog owners in the world (for a suitable value of n).

ASSUMPTION:

Suppose 2 to be false.

The assumption explicitly requires us to replace 2 by not-2: "Cats are not available." In the face of this supposition, we must abandon either 1 or 3 if consistency is to be maintained. For 1 and not-2 combine to yield the conclusion that the number of dog owners would *increase* beyond its present size, and this is incompatible with 3. But when—as usual—we prioritize general tendencies over specific facts, we shall arrive at the counterfactual in question. No recourse to nonexistent worlds is required to make good sense of this counterfactual. It is quite enough to take out real-world actualities and the relations of epistemic priority or precedence that obtain among them.

It is necessary in this context to distinguish between *world-altering* counterfactuals and *world-replacing* ones. The former takes the generic format:

If the world were F, then . . .

Here we have such instances as: "If large mammalian species had evolved much earlier, then fewer organic species would exist today," or "If the big bang had resulted in a hotter plasma, stable chemical elements would not have come into being," or "If the law of gravitation were an inverse cube law so that gravitation were a much weaker force, then there would be far fewer planetary systems with potentially life-supporting planets." Such hypothetical modification of the actual world leave enough in place that coherent inferences can be drawn from them.

However, the situation is very different with world-replacing hypotheticals of the format:

If a world entirely different from this one existed in its place, then . . .

In the wake of *such* a hypothesis—one that replaces this world by something altogether different—no coherent conclusion can be drawn. Once we envision that radical change, all cognitive bets are simply off; we are now at sea with no compass and no idea which way to turn. That radical world-abrogating hypothesis leaves us adrift on a sea of incomprehension. Any prospect of drawing a meaningful conclusion is denied us. The challenge of specifying an *alteration in* the actual world is producible for us, but that of specifying a *replacement for* the world—a genuinely alternative possible world—is beyond our powers. The conjunction "Keep as is only what you are explicitly instructed to maintain, and consider everything else as open to change." Here we just don't have a clue as to how to carry out this instruction, though. Changing *everything*—or even merely everything else—is simply too much for us. In this sort of situation the resources required for a meaningful process of counterfactual reasoning are denied to us.

But while we cannot come to satisfactory cognitive grips with "nonexistent possible *worlds*," we can indeed reason quite well from more concretely limited counterfactual suppositions. To do so, we need not look outside this world of ours to other possible worlds, but only inside to the epistemic priority status of our cognitive commitments. What we are called on to do is simply to make a comparative determination of post-assumption retainability among real-world truths. There is, fortunately, no need to enter into the problematic contemplation of the actuality of other, nonexistent worlds of which—if the preceding arguments hold good—we cannot really make proper sense. A recourse to the epistemic priorities that govern our commitments regarding our claims about the world is quite sufficient to deal satisfactorily with counterfactuals.

Fortunately, however, counterfactuals need not carry the crushing weight of possible worlds on their back. As we have seen, the crux of counterfactual analysis is not a matter of scrutinizing the situation in other possible worlds, but at most one of prioritizing our accepted beliefs regarding this actual one. There is simply no need to look beyond the cluster of the environing propositions that are immediately relevant to the particular counterfactual at issue. We certainly have no need to become involved in anything as grandiose as a possible world: dealing with a very moderate sector of reality suffices for all our needs. Counterfactual reasoning is a cognitively crucial device that neither demands nor invites an outlandish ontology of other possible worlds. And in particular, causal counterfactuals on the order of "If Susan had dropped the vase it would have broken" are obviously facts about the real world—it's just that they are facts about its *modus operandi* rather than about its occurrences and events.[18]

The key fact is that a recourse to nonexistent possible worlds is just not necessary for the semantics of modal logic because scenarios can take their place with equal effectiveness and greater conceptual economy. And it now emerges that possible worlds are also not needed for the analysis of counterfactuals. Accordingly, the idea that possible worlds must be accepted in semantical theory because of their explanatory indispensability in relation to modal and counterfactual propositions and inferences is simply fallacious. Indeed such an account brings in its wake a host of difficulties that obscure rather than elucidate the issues.

William Lycan has rightly observed that "we 'understand' counterfactuals in ordinary conversation, but for purposes of serious philosophy they have proved to be among the most troublesome and elusive expressions there are."[19] However, this seems to be the case only because recent philosophers have insisted on making matters difficult for themselves by bringing possible worlds into it. The fact is that the analysis of counterfactuals is at most a matter of a very localized propositional prioritization in line with some rather straightforward and pragmatically cogent rules. Given such right-of-way prioritization, the mystery of troublesome elusiveness is completely dissipated. And vast manifolds such as worlds do not come into it at all. As with an Agatha Christie detective story, a closer scrutiny of the proximate suspects immediately involved in the context at issue will suffice to resolve the mystery. In the interpretation and analysis of counterfactuals there is simply no need to look beyond the cluster of propositions immediately relevant to the particular counterfactual at issue, and certainly no need to become involved in anything as grandiose as an alternative possible world. Here, as elsewhere, recourse to possible individuals and possible worlds can be averted without significant loss.

All that is ever required for the analysis of counterfactuals is a handful of plausible ground rules of precedence and priority to settle matters of conflict resolution—of "right-of-way" in a conflict of aporetic inconsistency among the immediately involved reality-appertaining propositions. And operating in this way does not call for any *global* device of the sort at issue with possible worlds; all we ever need is a *local* device for assessing the comparative priority of a few propositions. The validation of counterfactuals and the assessment of their appropriateness certainly is merely matter of precedence and priority among the relevant beliefs that are at work in the setting of particular questions. What is at issue is a localized microprocess and not a globalized macroprocess: belief-contravening suppositions do not shift the frame of reference to other possible worlds but merely test the comparative solidity and staying power of our actual claims in the immediate contextual neighborhood. To have recourse to a metrically structured manifold of possible worlds to settle the questions of the assertability of counterfactuals would be like using a sledgehammer to squash a gnat. The pivotal lesson is thus clear: to validate counterfactuals as informatively productive assertions, we need not go so far as to launch conjectural global forays into other-worldly domains. It suffices to take note of the relevant local ground rules about the prioritization of claims in the setting of this actual one.

These deliberations about counterfactuals bear crucially upon the present topic of possibilia—possible worlds and objects. A merely possible individual or world as such is . . . nothing at all! What there is, is the *idea* of such an individual as it figures in a hypothesis or assumption: "Suppose there were a pink elephant in that corner of the hall" or "Suppose a kindly stranger gave you a pot of gold." Possibilia are hypothesis-correlative: they are the termini of supposition-claims. And what is basically at issue here is not *de-re*-wise an object as such but always merely a *de-dicto*-wise a proposition about such a (putative) object of the format: "Let it be supposed that *p*." For reasoning regarding such matters, we do not need to postulate an ontology of possibilities. All that we require is the standard machinery of a contrary-to-fact supposition and its consonant ground rules of precedent and contextual plausibility. In contemplating an ontology of possibility that proceeds on actualities alone (via available scenarios), we are not impoverishing the domain of the possible; we are enhancing that of the actual. Exactly that is the sort of thing that fiction does. And on this basis, an epistemic approach to counterfactuals can dispense with the mythology of possible worlds and enables us to encompass the domain of fancy and counterfact within the factual domain, and to enrich the realm of actuality with contemplations of possibility.[20]

▶ *Can Probabilities Help?*

Yet another variant approach to counterfactuals, one that proceeds on the basis of probability, has been proposed.[21] It is predicated on having at our disposal a manifold of quantified conditional probability values of the format $pr(p/q) = v$ for the relevant propositions. The idea now is to assess what would have happened if some falsehood *p* obtained by looking at the issue in terms of matters of conditional likelihoods relative to *p*.

Consider a simple schematic illustration of the operation of this approach. Suppose just three (independent) propositions are at issue. Then such a schedule of probabilities is equivalent to and can be represented as a distribution of likelihoods across the entire possibility spectrum as per display 4.1. Now let it be that the actual situation is as per case 3, so that *p* & ~*q* & *r* represents the truth of the matter. And let us then introduce a counterfactual assumption and inquire into what follows:

DISPLAY 4.1. A sample distribution of likelihoods

Case	*p*	*q*	*r*	*probability*
1.	+	+	+	2/16
2.	+	+	−	1/16
3.	+	−	+	3/16
4.	+	−	−	1/16
5.	−	+	+	4/16
6.	−	+	−	2/16
7.	−	−	+	2/16
8.	−	−	−	1/16

Note: The likelihoods of the last column are purely illustrative.

If not *p*, then??

On the postulated basis, the presently contemplated probabilistic procedure would proceed by examining the cases in which the projected hypothesis is realized, thereupon *accepting those conclusions that obtain in all of the maximally/sufficiently likely cases.* Thus in the present case we could either proceed on a maximum-likelihood standard to arrive at case 5 and thus have

If not-*p*, then *q* & *r*

or alternatively we could proceed on a sufficient-likelihood standard, thus eliminating the minimal-probability case 8 and arriving disjunctively at cases 5, 6, and 7, thereby validating:

If not-p, then $q \lor r$

Such an approach may seem promising from a formalistic point of view. Its fatal flaw, however, lies in the impracticability of implementing such a procedure in actual practice. For how on earth could we ever come to grips on such a probabilistic basis with:

If Columbus had not discovered America, somebody else would have.

For one thing, the project of surveying that entire spectrum of all theoretically available hypothesis-conforming possibilities becomes hopelessly formidable in any real-life application. But more serious yet is the question of those probability values. To be sure, the calculus of probability tells us how to conjoin with those probabilities once we have them. But where are they to come from and how are they to be determined? In the realistic cases that concern us there is no hope of securing the needed information.

Other serious problems also arise. For the whole project bears the ominous onus of a venture in elucidating something obscure in terms of something that is even more obscure than the target of our initial concern. We want to know if it is in order to answer questions of the format

If X were the case (which it is not), then would Y be so?

But in addressing this question we are sent off on the treasure hunt for answers to various questions of the following format:

If X were the case (which it is not), then how likely would it be for Y to be so?

It does not take much to see that proceeding in this way is to resolve one difficulty in terms of another yet more deeply problematic.

But perhaps the most telling argument against a probabilistic treatment of conditionals is that the features that standardly define conditionalization as such (*modus ponens*, transitivity, and the rest) generally fail to hold for probabilistic relationships. Accordingly, the approach to conditionals taken here takes an altogether different line in its insistence on coordinating conditionality with inferential processes.

▶*Impossible Counterfactuals*

One group of issues that manifests alike the factuality of a possible world approach to counterfactuals and a practicalistic approach is afforded by impossible counterfactuals. It is a decisive drawback and deficit of both of these approaches to counterfactuals that this range of cases cannot be accommodated.

For consider once more the preceding example: "If four were greater than five, then arithmetic would be involved in a contradiction." We clearly cannot handle this by contemplating the situation in those possible worlds where four is greater than five, since there obviously are not any. Nevertheless, no one would have any difficulty making sense of that counterfactual, and in fact the present aporetic analysis validates it straightforwardly. For in the setting of our current approach, we have the following accepted propositions:

1. Four is *not* greater than five.

2. The consistency of arithmetic (as we know it) entails 1.

3. Arithmetic is—and ought to be—consistent.

When not-1 is assumed, then we are at once forced into an abandonment of either 2 or 3, seeing that the trio {not-1, 2, 3} is logically inconsistent. Since there is no viable way around 2, this means that we will have to give up 3 and see arithmetic as involved in contradiction. And this validates the counterfactual under consideration. A possible world analysis, by contrast, could get nowhere here.[22]

We clearly cannot handle this by contemplating the situation in those possible worlds where four is greater than five, since there obviously are none. Nevertheless, no one would have any difficulty making sense of that counterfactual, and in fact the present aporetic analysis validates it straightforwardly.

Again, consider: "If there were twice as many integers between two and five as there in fact are, then there would be five integers between two and six." This too is smoothly amenable to our world-dispensing analysis. Consider:

ACCEPTED THESES:

1. There are two integers between 2 and 5 (namely 3 and 4).

2. There is one more integer between 2 and 6 than between 2 and 5, namely 5 itself.

ASSUMPTION:

Assume there to be twice as many integers between 2 and 5 as there actually are (namely, twice 2, as per accepted thesis 1).

The resolution here is straightforward. We must drop accepted thesis 1, as per the assumption. Moreover, we obtain four integers between 2 and 5—again as per the assumption. And between integers 2 and 6 we obtain one more, as per accepted thesis 2. This makes five integers in all, just as the counterfactual states.

Such impossibilistic counterfactuals create hopeless difficulties for a possible-world analysis. But the aporetic analysis of our current approach can accommodate them without difficulty.

5

The Aporetics of
Counterfactual History

The primary aim of historical inquiry is to elucidate the past—to describe and to explain the course of past events. Now in *describing* we are, of course, engaged in a strictly factual discussion. Here there is—or should be—little room for fanciful speculation: Leopold von Ranke's insistence that the historian's concern is with "how it actually was" (*wie es eigentlich gewesen war*) stands paramount. However, in moving beyond description to *explain* a course of historical events, it transpires that counterfactuals are an almost indispensably useful resource, and here aporetics once again comes to the fore. Thus we know perfectly well that (for example) "if Hitlerite Germany had developed an atomic bomb by 1943, World War II would have taken a very different course." What we have here is a *counterfactual conditional*: an answer to a question that asks what would transpire if, where this antecedent is false—or thought to be so. Such conditionals pivot on unrealized possibilities—such as Napoleon's remaining on Elba or Nazi Germany's developing an atomic bomb.

Along these line, the distinction between falsifying and truthifying causal counterfactuals is particularly significant in the context of historical issues:

> Falsifying case: If something-or-other—which actually did happen—had not happened, then certain specifiable consequences would have ensued. (Example: If the ministers of George III had not taxed the colonies, the American Revolution would have been averted in 1776.)

> Truthifying case: If something-or-other—which did not actually happen—had happened, then certain specifiable consequences would have ensued. (Example: If the American colonies had remained subject to Britain, control of the British Empire eventually would have shifted from London to North America.)[1]

With that first, falsifying example we have a situation of the following sort:

SALIENT BELIEFS:

p: George III's ministers taxed the American colonies.

q: The American colonies revolted in 1776.

Without p we would have not-q: not-$p \Rightarrow$ not-q: The American Revolution of 1776 was in substantial measure a response to George III's ministers taxing the colonies.

HYPOTHESIS:

not-p

Overall, we now confront the following situation:

> Assume not-p in the face of the aforementioned beliefs: p, q, not-$p \Rightarrow$ not-q. The problem then is that even after dropping

p, we must come to terms with the inconsistency of the group: not-p, q, not-$p \Rightarrow$ not-q.

And so here our supposition of not-p constrains a choice between the specifically factual q and the relational not-$p \Rightarrow$ not-q.

By contrast, in the second, truthifying example we have a situation of the following sort:

SALIENT BELIEFS:

not-p (The American colonies did not remain subject to Britain.)

q (Control of the British Empire has remained in London rather than North America.)

Since q then not-p: $q \Rightarrow$ not-p. (The retention of North America eventually would have disestablished the primacy of London.)

HYPOTHESIS:

p

And so here we have the situation:

Assume p in the face of those specified beliefs: not-p, q, $q \Rightarrow$ not-p. The problem then is that even after dropping not-p, we must come to terms with the inconsistency of the group: p, q, $q \Rightarrow$ not-p.

In short, our supposition constrains a choice between the specifically factual q and the relational $q \Rightarrow$ not-p.

Thus in both cases alike we must choose between a categorical and a relationally conditional fact. And as long as we prioritize comparatively more general relationships (conditional relationships included) over more restrictedly particular claims on grounds of informativeness, we must in both cases abandon the former and accept the latter in its place. In their logical structure the two cases are thus very similar, although they differ quite significantly in other respects.

Historical counterfactuals of the falsifying type—"if such and such had not happened"—generally address the *preconditions* for an actual occurrence—its temporally antecedent requisites. They are in general *retrospectively cause determinative* in nature. And this sort of thing is—or ought to be—grist for history's mill, given the explanatory mission of the enterprise. (It should be noted that counterfactuals of regret along the lines of "If only I had not done *X* but had done *Y* instead, I would not be in the mess I'm in today" are in effect historical counterfactuals in this retrospectively cause-determinative variety.)

By contrast, historical counterfactuals of the truthifying type— "if such and such had occurred"—generally address the *consequences* of a purely hypothetical event. They are in general *prospective* and *speculatively consequence determinative* in nature. This sort of thing is historically far more problematic, given history's intimate linkage to the world's actualities.[2]

With both of these types of counterfactuals we enter into the virtual reality of a suppositional realm of *"what if,"* but in the second, truthifying case we generally skate on much thinner ice. For the unrealism of the former, cause-oriented type of historical counterfactual is less severe than that of the latter, consequence-oriented type. The actual causal course of events now fades into the background, and it is the presumptive consequences of merely suppositional, actually nonoccurent events that now concern us. In sum, while falsifying counterfactuals remain within the orthodox bounds of a reality-based causal analysis—since in looking to the causes of actual eventuations we are still in effect concerned with how things have actually happened—truthifying counterfactuals, by contrast, are naturally more speculative and conjectural.

Temporal Asymmetry

Several recent writers have deliberated about the time direction at issue with counterfactual conditionals, being concerned that past-directed counterfactuals pose special difficulty.[3] The current approach can come to grips with these issues in a straightforward way. Thus consider a journey of successive daily stages along the following path:

A   B   C

Here there is clearly no difficulty with:

If the traveler were at B today (rather than at C, as is actually the case), then he would have been at A yesterday.

By contrast, suppose that the path system were to have a backward-forked pathway structure where several routes to a given destination are at issue as per:

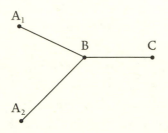

Now we can do no better than:

If the traveler were at B today (rather than at C, as is actually the case) then he would have been either at A_1 or at A_2 yesterday.

In other words, the question, "Where would the traveler have been yesterday if he were at B today rather than at C?" is now one to which—in the informative circumstances at issue—we simply cannot provide a definitely univocal answer.

On the other hand, suppose that the path system were:

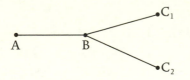

Now we cannot definitely answer the question, "If the traveler were at B today, rather than at A, as is actually the case, then where will he be tomorrow?"

Since the role of chance in our world is so structured that there are fewer causal convergent paths from the past than divergent causal paths to the future, it emerges that past-oriented ("backward-looking") counterfactuals will be in a more tractable condition than future-oriented ("forward-looking") ones. The situation of counterfactuals in relation to time order is thus destined not to be symmetric. The life of the historian is easier than that of the seer.

▸Examples

Counterfactual historical suppositions occur not only with claims about specific occurrences (events), but also with claims regarding general trends and tendencies (connected courses of events). And in resolving all such counterfactuals, the rule—as usual—is to prioritize informativeness.

Consider the counterfactual:

> If the European component of World War II had been prolonged by six months or more, the United States would have used the atom bomb against Germany.

This counterfactual arises in a context where the following propositions qualify as accepted facts:

1. The European component of World War II ended in April 1945, rather than substantially later.

2. The United States did not have its atomic bombs ready for use until August 1945.

3. The United States did not use the atom bomb against Germany.

4. The United States developed the atom bomb primarily with a view of its use against Germany, and would have used it to end the war in Europe if required.

Note that even if we abandon 1 and replace it by its negation, we would still have a contradiction on our hands, since not-1 in combination with 2 and 4 contradicts 3. In effect we would be forced to choose between 3 and 4, as long as 2 remains in place as an indisputable fact, because the context of the problem set by the supposition of 1-abandonment is the history of that war and not the history of technology. And so the standard policy of prioritizing generalities over specific events and event complexes leads to the validation of the counterfactual stated earlier.

Again, consider the counterfactual:

> If France had not aided Britain's American colonies during their revolt, they would not have won their independence.

In this context, the following propositions may be taken as accepted:

1. France aided the American colonies (by way of financial and naval support).

2. The American colonies won their independence.

3. The financial and military resources of the American colonies were insufficient to conduct a long, seriously contested war against Britain without substantial foreign financial and military support.

4. Among the world powers of the day, only France was willing and able to lend the American colonies such support.

5. Only a long, seriously contested war could possibly gain independence for the American colonies.

Observe that with 1 deleted and replaced by its negation, we still have a contradiction, because not-1 when combined with 3–5 yields not-2. In effect, we must choose between 2 and 3–5. However, the statements at issue here differ significantly in their epistemic status. For while 1 and 2 concern particular historical facts, 3–5 concern systemic historical facts. And so in line with the general policy of informativeness priority, we come to the result that 2 must be abandoned. The counterfactual at issue becomes established on this basis.

Another plausible example of a falsifying historical counterfactual is:

If Wellington had lost at Waterloo, then Napoleon would not have been forced into (immediate) exile in St. Helena.

This admits of the following justificatory analysis:

ACCEPTED FACTS:

1. Wellington did not lose at Waterloo.
2. Wellington and Napoleon were opposed commanders at Waterloo.
3. Napoleon went into (immediate) exile.
4. Victorious commanders are not forced into immediate exile.

ASSUMPTION:

not-1; Wellington lost at Waterloo.

Even if we drop 1 in the wake of the assumption, we still have a contradiction. For this assumption together with 2 entails "Napoleon won at Waterloo," so that "Napoleon was a victorious commander." And this together with 4 yields not-3.

Given that 2 is not an issue here, our assumption of not-1 in effect forces a choice between 3 and 4. And when we prioritize general relationships over particular facts—as is standard in counterfactual situations—we will retain 4 so that 3 must be sacrificed. And on this basis that initial counterfactual becomes validated.

On the other hand, another plausible example of a truthifying historical counterfactual runs as follows:

If Julius Caesar had not crossed the Rubicon in revolt against the Roman republic, this republic would have endured far longer.

Here we have:

ACCEPTED FACTS:

1. Caesar crossed the Rubicon in revolt against the Roman republic.

2. Caesar's revolt destabilized the republic and rendered it unstable and untenable.

3. Without this modality and conditionality the republic would have endured far longer.

Assume not-1. Then by 2, Caesar's actions had not (would not have) rendered the republic unstable and untenable so that by 3 it would have endured longer. Here the conditional at issue follows simply from the hypothesis plus the limited register of salient facts.

As such illustrations show, maintaining consistency in the case of historical counterfactuals envisions a priority ranking of the by now familiar sort, geared to the principle of fostering informativeness via the successive prioritization of:

1. Generalizations, "laws," well-established general rules, well-confirmed causal relationships

2. Trends, established relations among events, connections among particular eventuations, coordinative either-or or if-then relationships

3. Specific, particular, concrete eventuations

As ever, it is large-scale informativeness that is the crux for counterfactual reasoning rather than concrete specificity, as is the case with factual deliberation. And so the priority situation in these *speculative* cases is exactly the reverse of the order of evidential security that obtains in the factual setting of *inductive* reasoning, where theory must give way to facts and more far-reaching theories than those that are more particular in their bearing. Specifically, historical counterfactuals are in the same boat as others in that they pivot on considerations of rational economy via a Principle of the Conservation of Information.

And so, the crucial point for present purposes is that historical counterfactuals can—whenever plausible—be accommodated readily and naturally by the general process of counterfactual analysis that has been set out in the preceding chapters.

▶ Conclusion

To be sure, many historical counterfactuals lie in the region intermediate between the implausible and the cognitively intractable. For historical counterfactuals, like counterfactuals in general, must rest on an enthymematic basis of background belief, and such beliefs may, of course, be disputable and controversial—and particularly so with evidentially murky historical matters. Thus consider once more the counterfactual:

If Oswald had not shot J.F.K., then no one would have.

The problem with this conditional is that its tenability requires us to have belief-warranted access to a body of information *B* of such a sort that, if conjunctively added to "Oswald did not shoot J.F.K.," it would warrant the conclusion "No one shot J.F.K." Now, at the very least, this information would have to assure that there was *not* waiting somewhere in the wings someone who would have shot J.F.K. had Oswald not done so. But how in the name of common sense could we ever ascertain this even if it were so. Such a claim may well be beyond the range of secure determinability and is thus bound to be controversial. Replaying the course of history to see how things would have turned out in such a case is usually problematic on grounds of missing or uncertain information. After all, many—and perhaps even most—historical counterfactuals involve issues that suffer from insufficient or debatable data, the sorts of speculations they present are all too often insubstantial, thus rendering difficult the retention prioritization that counterfactual analysis requires. This, no doubt, is the principal reason why historians have traditionally been reluctant to engage in this sort of discourse.

6

Paradoxes

Paradoxes are the very model of apories arising when we have a plurality of theses, each individually plausible in the circumstances but nevertheless in the aggregate constituting an inconsistent group. In this way, logical paradoxes always constituted aporetic situations. For viewed separately, every member of such a group stakes a claim that we would be minded to accept if such acceptance were unproblematic. But when all these claims are conjoined, a logical contradiction ensues.

Every era in the history of philosophy has seen a concern with paradoxes. To be sure, the pioneering Zeno of Elea (b. ca. 500 B.C.) never called his paradoxes by that name, and even Aristotle often referred to them simply as "arguments" (*logoi*), though he denounced them as fallacies (paralogisms, *paralogismoi*). Another term used by Plato and Aristotle for such phenomena was "sophisms" (*sophismata*)—though it is doubtful that the Sophists themselves would have employed this term to characterize their arguments. These anomalous reasonings or *apories* (*aporia*) concerned Aristotle in his *Sophistical Refutations*, and the Stoics also devoted much interest to this subject—not to speak of the Sceptics, to whose mill they brought much grist. The medieval schoolmen were also enthralled by paradoxes, and some of their principal thinkers wrote extensively on *insolubilia*, as they pessimistically characterized such puzzling modes of argumentation. Kant treated the cognate issues under the title *paralogisms* and *antinomies*. In the nineteenth century, however, the term "paradox" ultimately established itself as standard for the phenomena at issue. But even as a rose by any other name would smell as sweet, so it is that throughout this long history one and the same thing—paradoxical argumentation—has been at issue throughout. In this regard the same fundamental problems—and often the same standard examples—have preoccupied logically acute thinkers since the dawn of philosophy.

As the Sceptics of classical antiquity stressed, sensory illusion paradoxes occur in situations in which we cannot even "trust our own eyes," as in the well-known case of the straight stick that looks bent when held at an angle underwater. Sight tells us it is bent; touch insists that it is straight. Or again consider the situation of looking at a landscape over a fire or a hot radiator. The trees and buildings vibrate and shake, while nevertheless "we know perfectly well" that they are immobile. Here we confront a Sense-Deception Paradox, where one sense affirms what the others deny. In all such cases we have to make up our minds about how to resolve the inconsistency.

Since logical paradox arises through the collective inconsistency of individually plausible propositions, it is clear that the individual premises of a paradox must be self-consistent. (Otherwise, they could hardly qualify as plausible.) And this means that those self-inconsistent propositions that are commonly characterized as paradoxical have to be viewed in a larger contest before actual logical paradox ensues. Thus consider the following proposition:

N: It is never correct to claim that something is never the case. ("Never say never!")

To make manifest that an actual (logical) paradox is at issue here, we have to elaborate the situation as follows:

1. *N* makes tenable claims.
2. *N* is a statement of the "it is never the case" format.
3. If *N* is correct, then every statement of the "it is never the case" format is false.
4. *N* entails its own falsehood—by 2, 3.
5. *N* does not make a tenable claim—by 4, since no claim that entails its own falsehood is tenable.
6. 5 contradicts 1.

It is this expanded account that elaborates the contradiction to which *N* gives rise, rather than simply *N* itself, that represents the paradox at issue.

▸ Paradoxes Root in Overcommitment

Since paradoxes arise through a clash or conflict among our commitments, they are the product of cognitive overcommitment. We regard more as plausible than the realm of fact and reality is able to accommodate, as is attested by our falling into contradiction. Paradox thus roots in an information overload, a literal embarrassment of riches.

In confronting paradoxical inconsistency, we have no sensible alternative but to do something, to abandon or at least modify one or another of the theses involved in the collision. At this point there is a decisive difference between theoretical and practical contexts. In practical contexts there is a possibility of compromise—of effecting a division that enables us in some way and to some extent "to have it both ways," say to proceed *A*-wise on even days and *B*-wise on odd ones. But we cannot rationally do this with beliefs. In theoretical contexts we must choose—must resolve the issue one way or another.[1]

However, logic alone will not help us to choose how a conflict of inconsistency should be resolved. It does no more than tell us that we must forgo one of the claims, but it affords no hint as to which one. The best we can manage here is to accept two of our three conflicting theses—namely, 1 and 3, with the resulting estimate of 3; or 2 and 3, with the resulting estimate of 5; or 1 and 2, with the resulting estimate of 4. Which route shall we choose? Here we are simply at sea—unless and until we have some further guidance. For note that the moment we learn that one of our sources is less accurate or reliable than the others, a definite resolution is at our disposal.

Greek philosophers of a whimsical tendency were drawn to sophisms (*sophismata*) along the lines of the Paradox of the Horns (*keratinês*) discussed by the Megarian philosopher Eubulides of Miletus.[2] It was based on the following reasoning:

1. You have no horns.

2. If you have not lost something, you still have it.

3. You have not lost any horns.

4. Therefore: you (still) have horns. (From 2 and 3.)

5. 4 contradicts 1.

Here theses 1, 2, and 3 are all supposed to be factual truths. However, 2 of course obtains only under the proviso that the thing in question is something you have had in the first place. Seeing that this paradox rests on a presupposition that, as it stands, is simply false, it is readily resolved.[3]

Again the following Truth Paradox affords an instructive example:

1. Truth is a property of sentences and only of sentences.

2. Sentences are elements of human language.

3. Human language cannot exist without humans.

4. Truth cannot exist without humans.

Some philosophers are beguiled by this line of thought into accepting an anthropocentrism of truth: accepting 1–3, they insist that 4 must be abandoned. But there are big problems here. For the reasoning at issue fails to heed the distinction between sentences and statements (i.e., the information that sentences purport). Actually, it is false to say, as per 1, that truth appertains to *sentences* only: it is also a feature of *statements*. And if we substitute "statements" for "sentences" in the argument, then 2 fails. For while human-language sentences can express statements, the facts at issue with potentially true statements can—at least in theory—outrun the limits of human language.

▶ Plausibility and Presumption

Logic can tell us when our modes of reasoning are valid—how it is that when applied to truths they must lead to truths. But it does not—cannot—tell us that when applied to plausibilities, valid arguments cannot yield implausible (or even self-contradictory) conclusions. (After all, a conjunction is often less plausible than its conjuncts.) Logic thus provides no insurance against paradox. And the reason is simple. Paradox resolution requires a choice among alternatives for premise abandonment. But logic is value-free. It will dictate *that* we must make choices in the interests of consistency resolution, but not *how*. It can criticize our conclusions but not our premises. And so, as long as we are conjuring with plausibilities, the threat of paradox dogs our steps, irrespective of how carefully and cogently we may proceed in point of logic.

The long and short of it is that paradox management requires an extra- or supra-logical resource. For the way to restore consistency to an aporetic situation is to implement some sort of prioritization principle that specifies how, in a case of conflict, we should proceed in making some of the relevant claims give way to others. What is needed is a rule of precedence or right-of-way. Considerations of priority are needed for breaking the chain of inconsistency at its weakest link. The guiding ideas of this approach are accordingly two:

1. Paradoxes of the most diverse sorts can be viewed in a uniform way as resulting from an aporetic overcommitment

to theses that, albeit individually plausible, are nevertheless collectively incompatible.

And on this basis,

2. Paradoxes of the most diverse sorts can be resolved through a uniform process of weakest-link abandonment in view of the fact that some of the conflicting theses take precedence or priority over others.

And with this second point, considerations of epistemic evaluation—of priority determination—become an inevitable part of paradox management. This means that plausibility and presumption become the crucial considerations.

Plausible propositions play a very special role in the cognitive scheme of things. We feel free to make use of them as premises when working out answers to our questions. But their use in the setting of particular question-resolving contexts is not predicated on an outright and unqualified commitment to these propositions as true. For we know full well that we cannot accept all those plausibilities as truths, since this can and generally would lead us into contradiction.

Plausibilities are accordingly something of a practical epistemic device. We use them where this can render effective service. But we are careful to refrain from committing ourselves to them unqualifiedly and come-what-may. And we would, in particular, refrain from using them where this leads to contradiction. In sum, our commitment to them is not absolute but situational: whether or not we endorse them will depend on the context. To reemphasize: the "acceptance" that is at issue here represents no more than a merely tentative or provisional endorsement.

The shift from assertion-as-true to assertion-as-plausible offers us a degree of flexibility with the claims that we make. Thus consider the Exception Paradox, which centers on the contention that "All generalizations have exceptions." This leads to the following paradox:

1. All generalizations have exceptions	by hypothesis
2. 1 is true	by 1
3. 1 is a generalization	from 1, by inspection
4. 1 has exceptions	from 1, 3
5. Any generalization that admits exceptions is false	as a principle of logic
6. 1 is false	from 3, 4, 5
7. 6 contradicts 2	

Note, however, that this paradox is immediately dissolved when the thesis at issue in 1 is asserted not as true but merely as plausible. For then the inferential step from 1 to 2, which is essential to deriving the contradiction, is automatically invalidated.

Unfortunately, life being what it is, we cannot always get away with accepting the plausible outright because actual truth is something more selective and demanding than mere plausibility, seeing that plausibilities—unlike truths—can conflict both with truths and with one another. Distributively true statements are of course collectively true: we have $[T(p) \& T(q)] \Rightarrow T(p \& q)$. But this is emphatically not the case with plausible let alone with merely probable statements. For plausible (and probable) statements can come into conflict with one another, and thereby impel us into paradox.

Plausibility is in principle a comparative matter of more or less. Here it is not a question of yes or no, of definitive acceptability, but one of a cooperative assessment of differentially eligible alternatives of comparative advantages and disadvantages. We are attached to the claims that we regard as plausible, but this attachment will vary in strength, in line with the epistemic circumstances. And this fact has significant ramifications. For the idea of plausibility functions in such a way that in matter of deliberation regarding facts *presumption always favors the most plausible of rival alternatives.*

The plausibility tropism inherent in the principle of a presumption in favor of the most plausible alternative is an instrument of epistemic prudence. It amounts to the sort of safety-first approach that is known in decision theory and the theory of practical reasoning as a *minimax potential-loss strategy*. The guiding idea of such a strategy is to opt in choice-situations for that alternative which minimizes the greatest loss that could possibly ensue.[4] (The strategy is obviously different from an expected-value approach.) The presumption of veracity is fundamental to the way in which we draw cognitive benefit from our sources of information—human and instrumental alike, our own sensory instrumentalities included. Once we recognize and acknowledge an informative source as such, we stand prepared to take its declarations at face value until such time as problems come to view.

▶ Addressing Paradox Resolution via Priority Ratings

The general process at issue with paradox management is best conveyed via some particular examples, beginning with the Smashed Vase Paradox based on the contention "There's no real harm done by breaking the vase—after all, it's all still there." Now consider the theses:

1. If we smash the vase into bits, the vase no longer exists as such.
2. There is nothing to the vase over and above the mass of ceramic material that constitutes it.
3. When the vase is smashed, all the ceramic material that constitutes it still remains in existence.
4. By 2 and 3, the vase still remains in existence after it is smashed, contrary to 1.

Thus {1, 2, 3} constitutes an inconsistent triad. And 1 and 3 are both incontestable facts, while 2 is no more than a plausible-sounding principle. We thus have no alternative but to reject 2 as the weakest link in the chain of inconsistency, plausibility notwithstanding.

Here presumably we would say something like: "There is more to the vase than merely the ceramic material that constitutes it, namely the organization of that material into a certain sort of vase-shaped-like configuration." On this basis we reject 2 as untenable, notwithstanding its surface plausibility.

In paradox analysis it becomes crucial to list in detail all of the theses and principles that are essential to establishing the aporetic collection at issue. For until the links of that chain of inconsistency are all spelled out explicitly, it is not possible to determine with confidence where exactly is the proper place to break the chain. If we do not have all the links set out, we cannot determine which of them is the weakest.

With a view of this methodology, consider the Happiness Paradox of John Stuart Mill, which goes as follows:[5]

1. His own happiness is the natural end of any rational agent.

2. A rational agent will adopt whatever end is natural for a being of his kind.

3. Therefore (by 2 and 3), a rational agent will adopt his own happiness as an end.

4. A rational agent will only adopt ends that he can realistically expect to achieve by striving for their realization.

5. Therefore (by 3 and 4), a rational agent can realistically expect to achieve his own happiness by striving for its realization.

6. But it is a fact of life that rational people realize that they cannot expect to achieve their own happiness by striving for its realization.

7. 6 contradicts 5.

As regards the status of the propositions involved, Mill himself saw 1 and 2 as basic principles of rationality. And he accepted 6 as a crucial insight into human nature. But 4 is not more than a highly plausible supposition. The ranking of those four theses in point of precedence and priority would accordingly be as follows: [1, 2] > 6 > 4 (note that theses of equal priority are bracketed together). Accordingly, Mill deemed it necessary to abandon any unqualified endorsement of thesis 4, however plausible and sensible it may otherwise seem to be. For the pursuit of even unrealizable ends can—in certain circumstances—yield other incidental benefits. This example is typical, and the process of paradox resolution accordingly has the following generic structure:

1. Setting out the aporetic group at issue in the paradox at hand, via an inventory of the aporetic (collectively inconsistent) propositions involved, and exhibiting how the logical relations among them engender a contradiction

2. Reducing this inconsistent set to its inferentially nonredundant foundation

3. Making an inventory of the maximal consistent subsets (MCS) of the resulting aporetic cluster. And on this basis—

4. Enumerating the various alternatives for retention/abandonment combinations (R/A alternatives) through which aporetic inconsistency can be averted

5. Assessing the comparative precedence or priority of the propositions at issue

6. Determining which among the resultant R/A alternatives for consistency restoration is optimal in the light of these priority considerations

Again, consider the following aporetic cluster—the Paradox of Evil—from the domain of philosophical theology:[6]

Paradoxes are the very model of apories arising when we have a plurality of theses, each individually plausible in the circumstances, but nevertheless in the aggregate constituting an inconsistent group. In this way, logical paradoxes always constituted aporetic situations. For viewed separately, every member of such a group stakes a claim that we would be minded to accept if such acceptance were unproblematic. But when all these claims are conjoined, a logical contradiction ensues.

1. God is not responsible for the moral evils of the world as exemplified by the wicked deeds of us humans, his creatures.

2. The world is created by God.

3. The world contains evil: evil is not a mere illusion.

4. A creator is responsible for whatever defects his creation may contain, the moral failings of his creatures included.

5. By 1–3, God is responsible for the world as is—its evils included.

6. 5 contradicts 1.

Let us step back and consider the systemic standing or status of these contentions. Thesis 5 can be put aside as a consequence of others that carry its burden here. Thesis 3 comes close to qualifying as a plain fact of everyday-life experience. Theses 1 and 2 are (or could reasonably be represented as being) fundamental dogmas of Judeo-Christian theology. But 4 is at best a controversial thesis of moral theology, involving a potentially problematic denial that creatures act on their own free will and responsibility in a way that disconnects God from moral responsibility for their actions. We thus have the priority ranking [1, 2] > 3 > 4.[7] On this basis it is reasonable to take the line that one of these aporetic theses must be abandoned in this context. And it is easily 4 that should give way, seeing that only the R/A alternative 1, 2, 3/4 abandons a lowest-priority thesis.

By deleting the less plausible items from an aporetic cluster so as to restore it to consistency we *purify* it, as it were, in the dictionary sense of this term of "diminishing the concentration of less desirable materials." But note that those less desirable materials are not necessarily worthless. For even they themselves are, by hypothesis, supposed to be more or less plausible. Though of lowest priority in one context, a plausible thesis that is caught up in an aporetic conflict may nevertheless be able to render useful epistemic service.[8]

It is, of course, possible that some propositions of an aporetic cluster will not figure in the inconsistency that arises. Such "innocent bystanders" will stand apart from the clash of contradiction and thereby belong to every maximal consistent subset (and to no minimal inconsistent subset). For them priority does not matter: they will emerge as immune to rejection, irrespective of any rankings of procedure and priority.

Disjunctive Resolutions: Conflicting Report Paradoxes

To be sure, the preceding rules will fail to decide matters when several distinct R/A alternatives are equally eligible. We then come to the end of our preferential tether without reaching a unique result. When this occurs and further preferential elimination is impracticable, we must fall back on a *disjunctive* resolution. For then all that we can say is that one or another of those equally eligible alternatives must obtain. This sort of thing is rare among the familiar paradoxes but can of course happen.

The journey into paradox sometimes proceeds by way of dilemma. A dilemma-engendered paradox takes the following generic form:

1. If C, then P. [A given.]
2. If not-C, then Q. [A given.]
3. Either P or Q. [From 1, 2.]
4. Not-P. [P is by hypothesis unacceptable.]
5. Not-Q. (Q is by hypothesis unacceptable.]
6. 3 contradicts 4–5.

Here an unavoidable disjunction (either C or not-C) leads to an unacceptable result (either P or Q).

Thus consider the following as an illustration of a Dilemmatic Paradox: Suppose you borrowed ten dollars from Tom and ten dollars from Bob. On your way to repaying them, you are robbed of everything but the ten dollars you had hidden in your shirt pocket. By no fault of your own, you now face the following paradoxical dilemma:

1. You are obligated to repay Tom and Bob.
2. If you pay Tom you cannot repay Bob.
3. If you repay Bob you cannot repay Tom.
4. You cannot honor all your obligations: in the circumstances this is impossible for you. [By 1–3.]
5. You are (morally) required to honor all your obligations.
6. You are not (morally) required to do something you cannot possibly do (*ultra posse nemo obligatur*).

Here {1, 2, 3, 5, 6} form an inconsistent cluster. 1, 2, and 3 are supposedly fixed facts of the case. Both 5 and 6 are—or seem to be—basic general principles of morality. Accordingly, one of 5 and 6—or both—will be abandoned. We here have an instance of the objective situation contemplated above.

To be sure, instead of outright rejection, we could endeavor to save them in some duly qualified form, perhaps somewhat as follows:

5'. You are morally required to honor all your obligations—albeit only insofar as the circumstances of the case permit (provided those circumstances are not of your own making).
6'. You are not (morally) required to do something you cannot possibly do (provided the improbability at issue is not of your own making).

Subject to such qualifications, the paradox can be overcome through premise abandonment along the by now familiar lines.

Other examples of disjunctive solutions are forthcoming in the case of Conflicting Report Paradoxes. Thus suppose that three equally reliable contemporaneous polls report the following paradoxical result regarding how people stand on a certain issue of public policy:

	1	2	3
For	30%	55%	30%
Against	30%	30%	55%
Unwilling to respond	40%	15%	15%

Here polls 2 and 3 are incompatible: there is no way to redistribute the nonrespondents of these polls so as to bring them into accord. We must thus choose between 1, 2/3 and 1, 3/2 whose condition in point of retention/priority is identical. A disjunctive result, along the lines of 1 & [2 v 3] now ensues, suggesting the inconclusive conclusion: For, 30–70 percent; Against, 30–70 percent. As far as our polling information goes, the situation is simply a tie—even though this was perhaps not clearly apparent on first view. And this resolution is the best that we can achieve here, since we are caught up in a tie in point of retention priorities. (If we had reason to discount pole 2 or pole 3, the result would be quite different.)

▸*More on Comparative Prioritization and Plausibility*

The simplest way to eliminate an aporetic paradox is to determine that one or another of its essential premises is flat-out untenable by way of being either meaningless or false. Here falsity is simple enough, but meaninglessness is rather more complicated because there are significantly different routes to this destination. The *hermeneutically* meaningless is literal nonsense, unintelligible gibberish; the *informatively* meaningless is absurd and conveys no usable information; and the *semantically* meaningless is devoid of any stable truth status, so that here there can be no fact of the matter one way or the other. "Yellow weighs wooden tentacles" is hermeneutically meaningless: one can make no sense of it. "He drew a square circle" is informatively meaningless: it anomalously takes away with one word ("circle") what it gives us with another ("square"); we understand—sort of—what is being said but deem it absurd. Finally, "This sentence is false" is semantically meaningless: neither truth nor falsity can be ascribed to it.[9]

In principle, various different avenues can lead to meaningless statements: grammatical anomaly, definition conflict, category confusion, presupposition violation, and referential vacuity. The first two generally produce hermeneutic meaninglessness, the next two generally engender informative meaninglessness, and referential vacuity generally leads to semantic meaninglessness.

While meaninglessness is perhaps the gravest flaw a paradoxical premise can have, mere falsity is yet another, somewhat less grave failing. In this light, consider the example afforded by Moore's Paradox, which centers on the paradoxical nature of locutions of the form "The statement P is true but I do not believe it."[10] This contention conveys the useful lesson of a complexity of "acceptance." The problem here turns on the fact that we may be of two minds about some things: that there are some facts that we acknowledge as such with one side of our minds but nevertheless find them somewhere between hard and impossible to accept. ("I find it incredible that some Confederate generals eventually became generals in the U.S. Army," or "I find it incredible that a president of the United States could survive in office despite a widely publicized affair with a White House intern.") Moore thus emphasized the paradoxical nature of sentences of the form "P, but I do not believe that P" ("The entire physical universe was once smaller than the head of a pin, but I do not really believe it"). To be sure, there is, in general, no anomaly to the assertion "P, but X does not believe it." The difficulty arises only in one's own personal case. And, as Moore sees it, the difficulty roots in the conflict between what the speaker *implies* by his assertions and what he *states* therein, between what is implicit and what is explicit.

To formulate the paradox that arises here, let S be a statement of the form "P, but I do not believe that P." And now consider the following:

1. S makes a meaningful statement that conveys coherent information. (A plausible supposition.)

2. In making an assertion of the form "*P* but also *Q*," a speaker indicates by implication his acceptance of *P*. (A logico-linguistic fact.)

3. In making an assertion of the form "*P*, but I don't believe that *P*," a speaker overtly states his rejection of *P* (i.e., his nonacceptance thereof). (A logico-linguistic fact.)

4. It follows from 2 and 3 that in making a statement of the form "*P*, but I don't accept that *P*," a speaker contradicts himself by indicating both that he accepts *P* and that he rejects it.

5. 4 is incompatible with 1.

Under the circumstances, we have little alternative but to abandon 1. Assertions of the form "*P*, but I don't believe that *P*" are accordingly untenable in contexts of rational communication on grounds of self-contradiction.[11]

The paradox contemplated by Moore is thus dissolved, because one of its crucial premises—namely, 1—is simply untenable. For while paradoxical statements of the form *S* are perfectly intelligible (*hermeneutically* meaningful) and people doubtless do say that sort of thing, they are nevertheless not *informatively* meaningful—there is little or no usable information that we can manage to draw from them. (Perhaps a more generous reaction would be to say that people who say "*P*, but I do not believe it" are simply adopting a somewhat incautious shortcut to saying something like, "Though I know full well that *P*, I nevertheless still find it difficult to accept its being so," which is a perfectly meaningful and unproblematic assertion.)

However, not every paradox can be written off so conveniently by rejecting some key premise as false or, worse yet, meaningless. Most paradoxes resist dissolution by this strategy and require us to invoke considerations of comparative plausibility.

The plausibility of the contentions at issue is in general pivotal for conflict resolution. Thus consider the following:

1. All A's are B's.

2. This A is not a B.

If 1 is seen as a law of nature and 2 as a mere guess, then we must of course jettison 2 as circumstantially untenable. On the other hand, if 1 is seen as a mere theory—a *candidate* law of nature, as it were—while 2 reports the discovery of a patent fact of observation (e.g., the Australian black swan that counterinstances the thesis that "All swans are white"), then it is 1 that must be abandoned. Its priority rating is thus a matter not of what a proposition *says*, but of the epistemic status that it has in the larger scheme of things.

Assessments of right-of-way precedence and priority accordingly do not relate to the declarative *content* of those paradox-engendering propositions—a more probable or plausible proposition does not somehow *say* "I am more probable/plausible." Its precedence and priority ranking bears upon the systemic standing or status that we take a claim to occupy in the cognitive situation at hand. (Think here of the analogy of an axiom in mathematics or formal logic. Axiomaticity is not a matter of what the proposition *says*, but rather of its cognitive *status* or *standing* in the system of propositions at issue.)

A thesis is minimally plausible when it is *compatible* with what we take ourselves to know. Beyond that, plausibility depends on the extent to which we are committed to it through case-specific evidence or—alternatively—through the centrality of its position within our overall body of cognitive commitments. We would and should be reluctant to see as plausible a claim that did not qualify as probable in the epistemic circumstances at issue.

Consider an example of how plausible contentions can engender paradoxes. Optical illusions always engender mini-paradoxes. Take, for example, the illusion created by the stick that looks bent when held at an angle underwater. Here we have two reports.

1. The stick is bent. (As attested by sight.)

2. The stick is straight. (As attested by touch.)

The two reports are clearly incompatible. To resolve the incompatibility at issue with such Optical Illusion Paradoxes, we must, as usual, assess the *comparative* plausibility of the propositions involved. Thus since touch is more reliable than sight in matters regarding the shape of smallish things, we resolve the apory by making 1 give way to 2.

Again, consider the optical illusion created when oppositely oriented arrowheads are put at the end of equal line segments.

A $\longleftrightarrow$
B $\succ\!\!-\!\!-\!\!-\!\!\prec$

Here we have the following:

1. Line segment A is shorter than B. (As reported by sight.)
2. Line segment A and B are equally long. (As reported by measurement.)

Since measurement is generally more reliable in such matters than sight, we can straightforwardly resolve this apory in favor of 2.

In this way, all optical illusions give rise to aporetic situations that can be resolved through preferential prioritization on the basis of larger background considerations regarding the plausibility of claims.

Comparative plausibility is our principal guide to paradox resolution. But in deliberation, as in life, damage control is generally not to be realized free of charge. When the propositions that we abandon are meaningless or false, their abandonment is effectively cost-free. But not so with plausible propositions. Clearly the more plausible a thesis is, the greater the price of its abandonment. In forgoing a plausible thesis we always lose something we would (ideally) like to have. And when this must be done for want of a cost-free alternative, we have to view the loss we sustain as the price of the best-available bargain. The aporetics of paradox-resolution is never an altogether painless process.[12]

Philosophical Aporetics

▶How Apories Pervade Philosophy

The big issues of philosophy regarding truth, justice, meaning, beauty, and the like were encapsulated in Immanuel Kant's summary of the key questions regarding one's place in the scheme of things as a rational free agent:

What can I know?

What shall I do?

What may I hope?

What should I aspire to?

However, thanks to the inherent complexity of the issues, the elaboration and substantiation of answers to such questions inevitably result in contentions that become enmeshed in aporetic conflicts. We have many and far-reaching questions about our place in the world's scheme of things and endeavor to give answers to them. Generally, the answers that people incline to give to some questions are incompatible with those they incline to give to others. (We sympathize with the sceptics, but condemn the person who doubts in the face of obvious evidence that drowning children need rescue.) We try to resolve problems in the most straightforward way. But the solutions that fit well in one place often fail to square with those that fit smoothly in another. Cognitive dissonance rears its ugly head and inconsistency arises. And the impetus to remove such puzzlement and perplexity is a prime mover of philosophical innovation. So, while philosophizing may "begin in wonder," as Aristotle said, it soon runs into puzzlement and perplexity.[1]

The doctrinal positions of philosophy standardly root in apories—in groups of individually plausible but collectively incompatible contentions. Just here, for example, lay the basic methodological insight of Plato's Socrates. His almost invariable procedure was a process of Socratic questioning to elicit a presystemic apory that sets the stage for philosophical reflection. Thus in the *Republic*, Thrasymachus was drawn into acknowledging the aporetic triad:

1. What men call *justice* is simply what is decreed by the authorities as being in their own interest.

2. It is right and proper (obligatory, in fact) that men should do what is just.

3. Men have no obligation to do what is in the interest of the authorities, particularly since those authorities may well themselves be mistaken about what these interests really are.

After all, the problem context of philosophical issues standardly arises from a clash among individually tempting but collectively incompatible overcommitments. Philosophical issues that standardly center about a family of plausible theses that is assertorically *overdeterminative* in claiming so much as to lead into inconsistency.

Or consider another example. Ordinarily, we would say that a person might have acted differently from the way he did, and, had he done so, would still be the very same individual. But Spinoza flatly denies that this is true for God and substantiates this claim by a thought experiment:

[It is wrong to say] that God can change his decrees. For if God's decrees had been different from what in fact he has decreed concerning Nature—that is, if he had willed and thought differently concerning Nature—then he would necessarily have had a different intellect and a different will from that which he actually has [and so would not be the being he is].[2]

With God, as Spinoza sees it, a change of mind would mean having a different mind and thereby being a different being. And of course since God (as Spinoza sees it) could not possibly be a being different from the one he is, this argumentation is to be seen as a *reductio ad absurdum* of God's decrees—and thereby the actual world—being different in any respect.

In addressing philosophical apories in the light of experience, the standard policy proceeds by breaking the chain of inconsistency at its weakest link. And in the setting of philosophical concerns, this will be a matter of weakness in point of assessed *plausibility*. This issue of philosophical plausibility will here be a matter of consonance with one's fundamental commitments, which is—and is bound to be—a matter of experience. The sort of data that a philosopher's course of experience has brought his way is going to be pivotal in this regard.

In these cases of collective inconsistency, something obviously has to go. Whatever favorable disposition there may be toward these plausible theses, they cannot be maintained in the aggregate. We are confronted by a (many-sided) cognitive dilemma and must find a way out. It is clear in these aporetic cases that *something* has gone amiss, though it may well be quite unclear just where the source of difficulty lies. The resolution of such an aporetic situation obviously calls for abandoning one (or more) of the theses that generate the contradiction. Unexceptionable as these theses may seem, one or another of them has to be jettisoned in the interests of consistency. And the problem is that there are always alternative ways of doing this. After all, the root cause of such a situation lies in cognitive overcommitment. Too many jostling contentions strive for our approbation and acceptance. And this state of affairs is standard in philosophy and represents the most common and pervasive impetus to philosophical reflection.

We could, in theory, simply suspend judgment in such aporetic situations and abandon the entire cluster, rather than trying to localize the difficulty in order to save what we can. But this is too high a price to pay. By taking this course of wholesale abandonment we lose too much through forgoing answers to too many questions. We would curtail our information not only beyond necessity but beyond comfort as well, seeing that we have some degree of commitment to all members of the cluster and do not want to abandon more of them than we have to.

Again, consider the following trio, which constitutes yet another aporetic cluster:

1. Taking a human life is morally wrong.
2. The fetal organism living in its mother's womb embodies a human life.
3. Abortion (i.e., taking the life of a fetal organism living in the mother's womb) is not morally wrong.

Here, too, the demands of consistency call for sacrificing something. And three alternatives present themselves:

Deny 1: Regard human life as expendable in certain circumstances; abandon the idea that it is sacred.

Deny 2: Gerrymander the idea of human life so as to exclude fetuses (perhaps only those that have not yet attained a certain state of development).

Deny 3: Condemn abortion as morally wrong.

In such situations, the issue is always one of a choice among alternatives where no matter how we turn, we find ourselves having to abandon something that seems to be plausible—some contention that, circumstances permitting, we would want to maintain and whose abandonment makes a great deal of difference.

Thus consider the following philosophical apory about freedom of action:

1. People are free agents: they can and sometimes do act from free choice.

2. If an action issues from free choice, then it is causally unconstrained.

3. All occurrences, human actions included, are caused—that is, causally construed—by antecedent occurrences.

Now since rejecting a thesis is tantamount to endorsing its negation, and the negation of a philosophically relevant contention is itself philosophical in its bearing, it follows that the pursuit of mere logical consistency involves one in endorsing a philosophical position.

Given an aporetic cluster of this sort, there is on the one hand substantial reason to maintain all of these collectively incompatible theses, because each has much to be said for it. On the other hand, the bare demand of logical consistency requires the *elimination* of some of these theses. The whole of the cluster is too much—something has to give way. And this is exactly where philosophy starts: not only in curiosity but also in wonder and confusion—in puzzlement and paradox engendered by the inconsistency of our cognitive inclinations.[3] Curiosity enters in because we have questions about the world to which we seek answers. But confusion also enters because the answers we incline to give are never totally compelling—nor even, as they stand, fully compatible with each other. In answering our various questions about the world and our place within it, we come to undertake commitments that engender overcommitment, so that we find ourselves plunged into perplexity.

Consider the just-stated apory from this angle. The fact that an inconsistent triad is at issue means that one must adopt at least one of the following positions:

Reject 1: This represents a *determinism* that denies free choice.

Reject 2: The acknowledgment that free actions can be caused leads straightaway to a theory of *agent causation* (Kantian "causality of freedom"), as contrasted to nature causation (Kantian "causality of nature"). The resulting position is that of a *compatibilism* of freedom and causality.

Reject 3: This envelops a doctrine of *occurrence surdity* to the effect that some events are uncaused. The result is causal exceptionalism that sees some events as positioned outside the causal order.

Several significant lessons emerge from this illustration: (1) the inconsistency-avoidance that rationality demands here requires a philosophical commitment of some sort; (2) with apory-resolution there will always be a choice among different alternatives; and (3) the range of this choice is limited to within a discrete and narrowly confined domain.

Doing nothing is not a rationally viable option when we are confronted with a situation of aporetic inconsistency. Something has to give. Some one (at least) of those incompatible contentions at issue must be abandoned. Apories constitute situations of *forced choice:* an inconsistent family of theses confronts us with an unavoidable choice among alternative positions.

Confronted by an aporetic antinomy, we recognize that something must give way. We ought, perhaps, to prefer to take the easy way out and ignore the difficulties, concealing them in a comfortable ambiguity rendered harmless by benign fact. But the urge to understanding does not allow us to rest satisfied in convenient ignorance. In all such cases, we are driven to make choices. We cannot maintain everything as it stands. The strength and weakness at issue here is determined through optimal systematization—by preserving as much as one possibly can of the overall informative substance of one's cognitive commitments. Realizing that something has to give and that certain otherwise plausible conclusions must be jettisoned, we seek to adopt those resolutions that cause the least seismic disturbance across the landscape of our commitments.

And this calls for a deliberative process that invokes weighing the comparative costs and benefits of a series of mutually exclusive alternatives in the endeavor to identify that (or this) which offers the best balance of benefits over costs. Accordingly, the overall process that is called for here is a matter of cost-benefit optimization on the basis of thinking through the overall consequences of competing alternatives. This sort of thing is clearly a matter of thought experimentation. That is, we contemplate accepting—one by one—each of the available prospects in the overall speculation of possibilities and weigh out the resulting assets and liabilities on a comparative basis to determine the optimal resolution.

Empiricists thus find themselves boxed into difficulty by the following quartet:

1. All knowledge is grounded in observation (the key thesis of empiricism).

2 We can only observe matters of empirical fact.

3. From empirical facts we cannot infer values; ergo, value claims cannot be grounded in observation (the fact/value divide).

4. Knowledge about values is possible (value cognitivism).

There are four ways out of the bind of this cycle of inconsistency:

Reject 1: There is also a nonobservational—namely, intuitive or instinctive—mode of apprehension of matters of value (intuitionism, moral-sense theories).

Reject 2: Observation is not only sensory but also affective (sympathetic, empathetic). It thus can yield not only factual information but value information as well (value sensibility theories).

Reject 3: While we cannot *deduce* values from empirical facts, we can certainly *infer* them from the facts, by various sorts of plausible reasoning, such as inference to the best explanation (values-as-fact theories).

Reject 4: Knowledge about values is impossible (positivism, value scepticism).

Committed to 1, empiricist thinkers thus see themselves driven to choose between the three last alternatives in developing their positions in the theory of value.

Again, consider the following epistemic apory.

1. Knowledge of matters of contingent fact is sometimes available: some such facts are known. (Fact cognitivism.)

2. Knowledge of matters of contingent fact cannot be based on abstract reasoning alone: it requires recourse to experience. (Empiricism.)

3. All human cognitive experience is potentially fallible, liable to error and malfunction. Experience can therefore never provide absolute certainty. (Experiential fallibilism.)

4. Knowledge must be absolutely certain. (Knowledge certitude.)

Here 2–4 entail that empirical knowledge is unavailable. This contradicts 1.

Reject 1: Fact scepticism.

Reject 2: Cognitive rationalism.

Reject 3: Experiential certitude: a theory along the lines of Stoic catalepsies.

Reject 4: Attenuated cognitivism (knowledge fallibilism).

This aporetic situation establishes a relationship among the philosophical doctrines: at least one of the four positive alternatives must be rejected; and at least one of the four negative counterparts must be accepted. And seeing that, all negation is determination, as Spinoza put it, the rejection of each of those propositions caught up in that natural aporetic conflict amounts to a substantive doctrine of some sort.[4]

Throughout speculative philosophy every position is surrounded by a penumbra of others that are collectively inconsistent with it. And there is a straightforward and cogent reason for this circumstance. For the answers to our philosophical questions always admit of plausible alternatives. After all, a contention whose denial has nothing whatever to be said for it is not worth such serious—let alone philosophical—consideration. So there are always tensions. And in consequence philosophical arguments can standardly be transmuted into aporetic clusters and analyzed in this light. Instead of proving a conclusion from "given" premises, what we have is simply a collection of variously plausible theses that are collectively inconsistent.[5]

We can thus subject philosophical issues to the standard process of aporetic analysis. For the contradiction that arises from overcommitment may be resolved by abandoning any of several contentions, so that alternative ways of averting inconsistency can always be found. A necessity for choice is forced by the logic of the situation, but no one particular outcome is rationally constrained for us by any considerations of abstract rationality. There are forced *choices* but no forced *resolutions*.

Apories Pervade the Philosophical Landscape

Consider the following passage in which Nietzsche contends (in effect) that, unlike prudence and the sense of self-advantage, conscience and the sense of moral wrong is a Johnny-come-lately in human history, something that is not deeply inherent in the human condition and therefore (presumably) something of little value for us.

1. For thousands of years, all evildoers overtaken by punishment would think, "Something has unexpectedly gone wrong here," and not, "I should never have done that."

2. They would undergo punishment as one undergoes sickness or misfortune or death, with that stout, unrebellious fatalism that still gives the Russians an advantage over Westerners in the management of their lives.

3. If actions were "judged" at all in those days, it was solely from the prudential point of view.

4. There can be no doubt that we must look for the real effect of punishment in a sharpening of man's wits, an extension of his memory, a determination to proceed henceforth more prudently, suspiciously, secretly, a realization that the individual is simply too weak to accomplish certain things; in brief, an increase of self-knowledge.

5. What punishment is able to achieve, both for man and beast, is increase of fear, circumspection, and control of instincts.

6. Thus man is *tamed* by punishment, but by no means *improved*; rather the opposite.

What is to be said about the probative status of these several assertions? Clearly something like this:

1. 1 is (presumably) a historical report, a summary of the records of the past.

2. 2 and 3 are of the same general sort as 1: they are (presumably) historical reports once again.

3. 4 is by all appearances a plausible inference that we are invited to draw from the data provided by 1–3.

4. 5 is a verbal reformulation of the point at issue in 4.

5. 6 is a plausible inference in the light of 4 and 5.

The probative structure of this passage is accordingly a matter of drawing plausible conclusions from one's general reading of the historical situation. The tenability of this whole bit of philosophizing accordingly hinges on the adequacy of those historical summaries and on the cogency of those supposedly plausible inferences drawn from them. What this principally requires is a matter of consonance with a philosopher's fundamental commitments.

Accordingly, the claims and contentions offered in the course of articulating, explaining, and substantiating a philosophical position must be harmonious in part of their probative status with the substantive content of the contentions at issue. A systemic unification of commitments is the crux. Yet what sort of foothold can and do these have for their probative support? Just what is it in the way of cognitive commitments that is being harmonized? There is a wide range of possibilities here. In philosophical texts one encounters statements that represent:

- Self-certifying biographical avowals ("I dislike solving quadratic equations")
- Parts of the mechanism of communication ("Let p stand for 'Today is Tuesday' and q for 'Tomorrow is Wednesday'")
- Claims that are self-evident—or supposedly so ("It is easier to discern triangles than chiliagons")
- Matters of determinable empirical fact ("People find it hard to accept that a day will come when they no longer exist")
- Common knowledge: things that any reasonably well-informed person can be expected to know ("People and animals require nourishment to live")
- Technical knowledge: things that technical experts come to realize and that we ought to accept on their authority ("Different people respond differently to the same medicaments")
- Commonsense beliefs, common knowledge, and what have been "the ordinary convictions of ordinary people since time immemorial"

- The facts (or purported facts) afforded by the science of the day; the views of well-informed "experts" and "authorities"
- The lessons we derive from our dealings with the world in everyday life
- Received opinions that constitute the worldview of the day; views that accord with the "spirit of the times" and the ambient convictions of one's cultural context
- Tradition, inherited lore, and ancestral wisdom (including religious tradition)
- The "teachings of history" as best we can discern them

These various commonplaces all constitute data for philosophizing. They are the fundamental commitments that constitute the foundation upon which sensible philosophizing must erect its theoretical structure. The possibilities here are in theory virtually endless, though in practice there are a modest number of predominant types along the lines of the just-indicated enumeration. And it is these types that both delineate the background against which philosophical thought experimentation proceeds and which set the stage for the reasonable-conformity deliberations required for the resolution of philosophy's aporetic problems.

These considerations indicate why and how it is that thought experimentation is so prominent an instrument to philosophical reasoning. For when confronted with a group of individually plausible but collectively inconsistent propositions, it is only natural and sensible to explore experimentally each of the various ways of restoring consistency through thesis abandonment and to consider in each case the balance of advantage versus disadvantage—of cost versions benefit, so to speak—of adopting this particular resolution. After all, no exit from aporetic inconsistency is cost-free—each requires us to give up something that—ideally—we would like to have.

Apories so function as to make manifest how various positions are interlocked in a mutual interrelationship that does not meet the eye at first view because the areas at issue may be quite disparate. Consider, for example, the following apory that arises in philosophical deliberation about facts and values:

1. All knowledge is based on observation. (Empiricism)

2 We can only observe matters of empirical fact. (Naturalism)

3. Knowledge about values is possible. (Value cognitivism)

4. We cannot infer values from empirical facts alone. (Axiological antinomy)

On first view, these theses seem altogether disparate and disconnected. They stem from regions separated by disciplinary divisions. Thus theses 1–3 are squarely epistemological, while 4 looks to be distinctly axiological. But their aporetic interrelationship puts matters into a very different light. For mere logic connects what disciplines put asunder.

Since theses 2 and 4 entail that value statements cannot be inferred from observations, we arrive via 1 at the denial of 3. Inconsistency is upon us. There are four ways out of this trap:

Deny 1: There is also nonobservational—intuitive or instinctive—knowledge of various kinds—specifically of matters of value (value intuitionism; moral-sense theories).

Deny 2: Observation is not only sensory but also affective (sympathetic, empathetic). It thus can yield not only factual information but value information as well (value-sensibility theories).

Deny 3: Knowledge about values is impossible (positivism, value skepticism).

Deny 4: While we cannot *deduce* values from empirical facts, we can certainly *infer* them from the facts, by various sorts of plausible reasoning such as "inference to the best explanation" (values-as-fact theories).

In connecting, for example, empiricism and fact-value separation, such an analysis brings to light significant interrelationships that obtain among disparate topics. It makes strange bedfellows of very different philosophical doctrines in exactly the way that we have been considering, interrelating issues that appear to be substantively disjointed and seem to belong to different disciplines (epistemology and axiology is the example).

Among the most familiar and historically significant apories are the familiar Kantian antinomies: coordinated pairs of arguments leading to mutually contradictory conclusions. His first antinomy, for example, proceeds effectively as follows:

A. The world is limited in space and time. Consider the following:

1. If the world were spatio/temporally infinite, its realization as a completed whole would require accomplishing an infinite process.

2. An infinite process can never be accomplished completely and in toto as a whole.

3. The world as we have it is a completed whole.

4. Since 2 and 3 combine to negate the consequent of 1, its antecedent must be denied, and A thereby seen as established.

B. The world is unlimited in space and time. Consider the following:

5. If the world were spatio/temporally limited, then time itself (being limited) must have a start, and space itself (being limited) must have an end.

6. The idea of a start to time is absurd.

7. The idea of an end to space is absurd.

8. Since 6 and 7 combine to negate the consequent of 5, its antecedent must be denied and thereby B seen as established.

But since theses A and B are mutually contradictory, it follows that contentions 1–3 plus 5–7 combine to form an aporetic group—and indeed one that combines such varied issues as the theory of process (as per 2) with the theory of nature (as per 3). Something is rotten in this reasoning's Denmark, and since the two conflicting arguments are effectively on a par, the whole issue of A versus B must be seen as problematic. As Kant saw it, the problem roots in seeing "the world" as an individual object that affords a suitable subject for predication. And an analogous story with the same upshot holds for the other antinomies as well.

An apory thus delineates a definite range of interrelated positions. It maps out a small sector of the possibility space of philosophical deliberation. And this typifies the situation in philosophical problem solving, where, almost invariably, several distinct and discordant resolutions to a given issue or problem are available, none of which our cognitive data can exclude in an altogether decisive way. Here any particular resolution of an aporetic cluster is bound to be simply *one way among others*. The single most crucial fact about an aporetic cluster is that there will always be a variety of distinct ways of averting the inconsistency into which it plunges us. We are not only forced to choose but also constrained to operate within a narrowly circumscribed range of choice.

Consider the following aporetic cluster of individually plausible but collectively inconsistent theses:

1. Human life is sacred: human beings should never be sacrificed to suit the mere convenience of others.

2. Yet unborn babies (i.e., sufficiently matured fetuses) qualify as human beings.

3. Women have a free (i.e., morally unfettered) right to terminate their pregnancies for whatever reasons they see fit (including their mere personal convenience).

The inconsistency that lurks here can be elicited as follows:

> By thesis 3 we can infer that women have a free right to terminate their pregnancies to suit their own personal convenience—that is, they are morally unrestrained in a decision about terminating their pregnancies.

From theses 1 and 2 it follows that unborn babies should never be sacrificed to the mere convenience of others, and that women are not morally unrestrained in a decision about terminating their pregnancies.

Theses 1–3 accordingly come into logical collision and present us with a forced option.

But note that what is at issue here is a group of theses from disparate domains. The theses belong to very different areas of philosophical discussion:

- Metaphysics: specifically the theory of ontological evaluation (in particular, the value of life in its humanoid configuration)
- Philosophical anthropology: specifically the theory of human nature
- Moral philosophy: specifically the theory of human rights

The logical inconsistency of those three contents in their collective interaction shows how theses from different domains enter into an interactive relationship with one another.

And this sort of cognitive phenomenology is typical of philosophical issues in general. The holistic unity of theoretical knowledge means that they interact across disciplinary boundaries through the mediation of aporetic conflicts. In philosophy, as elsewhere, all determination is negation. Every claim conflicts not only with its own denial but also with whatever complex or combination of claims has this denial as an inferential consequence. As a cognitive enterprise, philosophizing is invariably involved in a network of interlocking commitments, and when some of the strands are pulled others will be stretched and perhaps broken.[6] The aporetic nature of philosophy calls for the discipline being developed in a systematic manner.

On this basis, their grounding in aporetic conflicts provides philosophical controversies with a rational structure that endows its problem areas with an organic unity. The various alternative ways of resolving such a cognitive dilemma present a restricted manifold of interrelated positions—a comparatively modest inventory of possibilities mapping out a family of (comparatively few) alternatives that span the entire spectrum of possibilities for averting inconsistency.[7] And the history of philosophy is generally sufficiently fertile and diversified that all the alternatives—all possible permutations and combinations for problem resolution—are in fact tried out somewhere along the line.

Philosophical doctrines are accordingly not discrete and separate units that stand in splendid isolation. They are articulated and developed in reciprocal interaction. But their natural mode of interaction is *not* by way of mutual supportiveness. (How could it be, given the mutual exclusiveness of conflicting doctrines?) Rather, competition and controversy prevail. The search of the ancient Stoics and Epicureans (notably Hippias) for a universally "natural" belief system based on what is common to different groups (espousing different doctrines, customs, moralities, religions) is of no avail because no single element remains unaffected as one moves across the range of variation. Given that rival "schools" resolve an aporetic cluster in different and discordant ways, the area of agreement between them, though always there, is bound to be too narrow to prevent conflict. Alternative positions make different priorities, and different priorities are by nature incompatible and irreconcilable.

It emerges against this background how it is that an aporetic perspective or philosophizing comes to be significantly instructive: (1) We now see these propositions in their interrelational interconnectedness. We come to realize that they are related notwithstanding the prospect of a radical diversity of thematic subject matter.

(2) We are confronted in a very clear and urgent way with the need for choice insofar as it is truth that is our goal. (3) We get a clear view of the battlefield—and are able to pinpoint with enhanced precision and detail exactly where the discordances between alternative parties are located.

Other illustrations are readily available. A metaphysical determinism that negates free will runs afoul of a traditionalistic ethical theory that presupposes it. A philosophical anthropology that takes human life to originate at conception clashes with a social philosophy that sees abortion as morally unproblematic. A theory of rights that locates all responsibility in the contractual reciprocity of freely consenting parties creates problems for a morality of concern for animals. And the list goes on and on. In dealing with issues of the complexity and difficulty that philosophical problems generally involve, the tension of aporetic conflict is pretty well inescapable.[8]

The task of philosophy, as Socrates clearly saw, is to work our way out of the thicket of inconsistency in which we are entangled by our presystemic beliefs. For the sake of sheer consistency, something one might otherwise like to keep must be abandoned—or at least qualified. And when this happens, philosophizing becomes a matter of cost-benefit optimization relative to one's overall systemic commitments.

8

The Dialectics of
Philosophical Development

Plausibility aporetics affords some useful insight into the developmental dialectics of philosophy. Aporetics affords a means for not only mapping the cartography of the battlefield of philosophical disputation, but also understanding and explaining the dialectic of historical development in the field.

While securing answers to our questions is the aim of the philosophical enterprise, we do not want just answers but coherent answers, seeing that these alone have a chance of being collectively true. The quest for consistency is an indispensable part of the quest for truth. The quest for consistency is one of the driving dynamic forces of philosophy. But the cruel fact is that theorizing itself yields contradictory results. In moving from empirical observation to philosophical theorizing, we do not leave contradiction behind—it continues to dog our footsteps. And just as reason must correct sensation, so more refined and elaborate reason is always needed as a corrective for less refined and elaborate reason. The source of contradiction is not just in the domain of sensation but in that of reasoned reflection as well. We are thus impelled into philosophy by the urge for consistency, and we are ultimately *kept* at it by this same urge.

In breaking out of the cycle of inconsistency created by an aporetic cluster one has no choice but to abandon one or the other of the propositions involved. But in jettisoning this item it is often—perhaps even generally—possible to embody a distinction that makes it possible to retain something of what is being abandoned. Thus consider an illustration. We begin with four plausible contentions:

1. Every occurrence in nature is caused.

2. Causes necessitate their consequences.

3. Necessitation precludes contingency.

4 Some occurrences in nature are contingent.

Someone who decides to break the cycle of inconsistency by dropping thesis 3 might nevertheless distinguish causal necessitation and causal production, and in consequence maintain that what causes do not necessitate these effects may nevertheless produce them (albeit in ways that are not at issue with the contingency of the product). And this exemplifies a general situation. To restore consistency among incompatible beliefs calls for abandoning some of them as they stand. In general, however, philosophers do not provide for consistency restoration wholly by way of rejection. Rather, they have recourse to *modification*, replacing the abandoned belief with a duly qualified revision thereof. Since (by hypothesis) each thesis belonging to an aporetic cluster is individually attractive, simple rejection lets the case for the rejected thesis go unacknowledged. Only by modifying the thesis through a resort to distinctions can one manage to give proper recognition to the full range of considerations that initially led into aporetic difficulty.

Distinctions enable the philosopher to remove inconsistencies not just by the brute negativism of thesis *rejection*, but by the more subtle and constructive device of thesis *qualification*. The crux of a distinction is not mere negation or denial, but the amendment of an untenable thesis into something positive that does the job better. To examine the workings of this sort of process further, consider an aporetic cluster that set the stage for various theories of early Greek philosophy:

1. Reality is one (homogeneous).

2. Matter is real.

3. Form is real.

4. Matter and form are distinct sorts of things (heterogeneous).

In looking for a resolution here, one might consider rejecting 2. This could be done, however, not by simply *abandoning* it, but rather by *replacing* it—on the idealistic precedent of Zeno and Plato—with something along the following lines:

2'. Matter is not real as an independent mode of existence; rather, it is merely quasi-real, a mere *phenomenon*, an appearance somehow grounded in immaterial reality.

The new quartet (1, 2', 3, 4) is entirely cotenable.

Now in adopting this resolution, one again resorts to a *distinction*—namely, that between

i. Strict reality as self-sufficiently independent existence

and

ii. Derivative or attenuated reality as a (merely phenomenal) product of the operation of the unqualifiedly real

Use of such a distinction between unqualified and phenomenal reality makes it possible to resolve an aporetic cluster—yet not by simply *abandoning* one of those paradox-engendering theses but rather by *qualifying* it. (Note, however, that once we follow Zeno and Plato in replacing 2 by 2'—and accordingly reinterpret matter as representing a "mere phenomenon"—the substance of thesis 4 is profoundly altered; the old contention can still be maintained, but it now gains a new significance in the light of new distinctions.)

Again one might—alternatively—abandon thesis 3. However, one would then presumably not simply adopt "form is not real" but rather would go over to the qualified contention that "form is not *independently* real; it is no more than a transitory (changeable) state of matter." And this can be looked at the other way around, as saying "form *is* (in a way) real, although only insofar as it is taken to be no more than a transitory state of matter." This, in effect, would be the position of the atomists, who incline to see as implausible any recourse to mechanisms outside the realm of the material.

The exfoliative development of philosophical systems is driven by the quest for consistency. But once an apory is resolved through the decision to drop one or another member of the inconsistent family at issue, it is only sensible and prudent to try to salvage some part of what is sacrificed by introducing a distinction. Aporetic inconsistency can always be resolved in this way, seeing that we can always "save the phenomena"—that is, retain the crucial core of our various beliefs in the face of apparent consideration—by introducing suitable distinctions and qualifications. Once apory breaks out, we can thus salvage our philosophical commitments by *complicating* them, through revisions in light of appropriate distinctions, rather than abandoning them altogether. Yet all too often inconsistency will break out once more within the revised family of propositions that issues from the needed readjustments. And then the entire process is carried back to its starting point. The overall course of development thus exhibits the following overall cyclical structure:

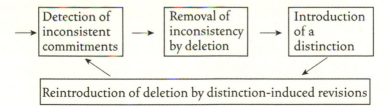

To be sure, the process of thesis revision in light of distinctions is not just a matter of clarification but also one of enhancing the acceptability (plausibility, tenability, truthfulness) of what has been retained.

The pivotal role of distinctions in aporetics has significant implications, for it highlights the circumstance that the aim of the enterprise is not simply the negative one of eliminating the troublemakers that engender inconsistency in our belief commitments. This business of deciding what must go is only the first negative phase in a complex dialectical enterprise that serves to set the stage for a second positive phase—namely that of exploring how much of what is being abandoned can be retained without readmitting inconsistency once more. It is just here that distinctions enter in to serve their indispensable function.

The historical course of philosophy often tracks an evolving process of apory resolution by means of distinctions. And this process of dialectical development imposes certain characteristic structural features upon the course of philosophical history:

Concept proliferation: ever more elaborate concept manifolds evolve.

Concept sophistication: ever more subtle and fine-drawn distinctions.

Doctrinal complexification: ever more extensively formulated theses and doctrines.

System elaboration: ever more elaborately articulated systems.

And so, the unfolding of distinctions has important ramifications in philosophical inquiry. As new concepts crop up in the wake of distinctions, new questions arise regarding their bearing on the issues. In the course of securing answers to our old questions, we open up further questions, questions that could not even be asked before.

▶*More on Distinctions*

The history of philosophy is replete with distinctions introduced to avert aporetic difficulties. Already in the dialogues of Plato, the first systematic writings in philosophy, we encounter distinctions at every turn. In Book I of the *Republic*, for example, Socrates' interlocutor quickly falls into the following apory:

1. Rational people always pursue their own interests.

2. Nothing that is in a person's interest can be disadvantageous to him.

3. Even rational people sometimes do things that prove disadvantageous.

Here, inconsistency is averted by distinguishing between two senses of the interests of a person—namely, what is *actually* advantageous to him and what he merely *thinks* to be so; that is, between *real* and *seeming* interests. Again, in the discussion of "nonbeing" in the *Sophist*, the Eleatic stranger entraps Theaetetus in an inconsistency from which he endeavors to extricate himself by distinguishing between nonbeing in the sense of not existing *at all* and in the sense of not existing *in a certain mode*. For the most part, the Platonic dialogues present a dramatic unfolding of one distinction after another.

And this situation is typical in philosophy. The natural dialectic of problem solving here drives us even more deeply into drawing distinctions, so as to bring new, more sophisticated concepts upon the scene.

To be sure, distinctions are not needed if *all* that concerns us is averting inconsistency; simple thesis abandonment, mere refusal to assert, will suffice for that end. One can guard against inconsistency by avoiding commitment. But such sceptical refrainings create a vacuum. Distinctions are indispensable instruments in the (potentially never-ending) work of rescuing the philosopher's assertoric commitments from inconsistency while yet salvaging what one can. They become necessary if we are to maintain informative positions and provide answers to our questions. Whenever a particular aporetic thesis is rejected, the optimal course is not to abandon it altogether, but rather to minimize the loss by introducing a distinction by whose aid it may be retained *in part*. After all, we do have some commitment to the data that we reject and are committed to saving as much as we can. (This, of course, is implicit in our treating those data as such in the first place.)

Of course any particular way out of an aporetic conflict is bound to be simply *one way among others*. The single most crucial fact about an aporetic cluster is that there will always be a variety of distinct ways of averting the inconsistency into which it plunges us. And in this light, the problem for the philosopher is not one of inductive ampliation but of systemic reduction—of a restoration of consistency through choices of priority. In general, to be sure, philosophers fail to reach a uniform result because this prioritization can in theory always be accomplished in very different ways. The crux is that different philosophers implement different priority systems in effecting such determinations about what must be made to give way. Any and every resolution of a philosophical antinomy represents a distinct—and distinctly different—position, an intellectual abode that someone caught up in the underlying apory may choose to inhabit, though sometimes no one does so.

A distinction accordingly reflects a *concession*, an acknowledgment of some element of acceptability in the thesis that is being rejected. However, distinctions always bring a new concept upon the stage of consideration and thus put a new topic on the agenda. And they thereby present invitations to carry the discussion further, opening up new issues that were heretofore inaccessible. Distinctions are the doors through which philosophy moves on to new questions and problems. They bring new concepts and new theses to the fore.

Distinctions enable us to implement the irenic idea that a satisfactory resolution of aporetic clusters will generally involve a compromise that somehow makes room for all parties to the contradiction.

The introduction of distinctions thus represents a Hegelian ascent—rising above the level of antagonistic doctrines to that of a "higher" conception, in which the opposites are reconciled. In introducing the qualifying distinction, we abandon that initial conflict-facilitating thesis and move toward its counterthesis—but only by way of a duly hedged synthesis. In this regard, distinction is a "dialectic" process. This role of distinctions is also connected with the thesis often designated as "Ramsey's Maxim." For with regard to disputes about fundamental questions that do not seem capable of a decisive settlement, Frank Plumpton Ramsey wrote: "In such cases it is a heuristic maxim that the truth lies not in one of the two disputed views but in some third possibility which has not yet been thought of, which we can only discover by rejecting something assumed as obvious by both the disputants."[1] On this view, then, distinctions provide for a higher synthesis of opposing views; they prevent thesis abandonment from being an *entirely* negative process, affording us a way of salvaging something, of giving credit where credit is due, even to those theses we ultimately reject. They make it possible to remove inconsistency not just by the brute force of thesis rejection, but by the more subtle and constructive device of thesis qualification.

Philosophical distinctions are thus creative innovations. There is nothing routine or automatic about them—their discernment is an act of inventive ingenuity. They do not elaborate preexisting ideas but introduce new ones. They not only provide a basis for understanding better something heretofore grasped imperfectly but shift the discussion to a new level of sophistication and complexity. Thus, to some extent they "change the subject." (In this regard they are like the conceptual innovations of science that revise rather than explain prior ideas.)

Philosophy's recourse to ongoing conceptual refinement and innovation means that a philosophical position, doctrine, or system is never closed, finished, and complete. It is something organic, ever growing and ever changing—a mere tendency that is in need of ongoing development. Its philosophical "position" is never actually that—it is inherently unstable, in need of further articulation and development. Philosophical systematization is a process whose elements develop in stages of interactive feedback—its exfoliation is a matter of dialectic, if you will.

▶A Historical Illustration

The inherent dynamic of this dialectic deserves a closer look. Let us consider a historical example. The speculations of the early Ionian philosophers revolved about four theses:

1. There is one single material substrate (*archê*) of all things.
2. The material substrate must be capable of transforming into anything and everything (and thus specifically into each of the various elements).
3. The only extant materials are the four material elements: earth (solid), water (liquid), air (gaseous), and fire (volatile).
4. The four elements are independent—none gives rise to the rest.

Different thinkers proposed different ways out of this apory:

- Thales rejected 4 and opted for water as the *archê*.
- Anaximines rejected 4 and opted for air as the *archê*.
- Heracleitus rejected 4 and opted for fire as the *archê*.
- The atomists rejected 4 and opted for earth as the *archê*.
- Anaximander rejected 3 and postulated an indeterminate *apeiron*.
- Empedocles rejected 1, and thus also 2, holding that everything consists in *mixtures* of the four elements.

Thus, virtually all of the available exits from inconsistency were actually used. The thinkers involved either resolved to a distinction between genuine primacy and merely derivative "elements" or, in the case of Empedocles, stressed the distinction between mixtures and transformation. But all of them addressed the same basic problem—albeit in the light of different plausibility appraisals.

As the pre-Socratics worked their way through the relevant ideas, the following conceptions came to figure prominently on the agenda:

I

1. Whatever is ultimately real persists through change.
2. The four elements—earth (solid), water (liquid), air (gaseous), and fire (volatile)— do not persist through change as such.
3. The four elements encompass all there is by way or extant reality.

Three basic positions are now available:

Abandon 1: Nothing persists through change—*panta rhei*, all is in flux (Heracleitus).

Abandon 2: One single elements persists through change—it alone is the *archê* of all things; all else is simply some altered form of it. This uniquely unchanging element is: earth (atomists), water (Thales), air (Anaximines), fire (Heracleitus). Or again, *all* the elements persist through change, which is only a matter of a variation in mix and proportion (Empedocles).

Abandon 3: Matter itself is not all there is—there is also its inherent geometrical structure (Pythagoras) or its external arrangement in an environing void (atomists). Or again, there is also an immaterial motive force that endows matter with motion—to wit, "mind" (*nous*) (Anaxagoras).

Let us follow along in the track of atomism by abandoning 3 through the distinction between material and nonmaterial existence. With this cycle of dialectical development completed, the following aporetic impasse arose in pursuing the line of thought at issue:

II

1. Change really occurs.

2. Matter (solid material substance) does not change, nor does vacuous emptiness.

3. Matter and the vacuum is all there is.

As always, different ways of escaping from contradiction are available:

Abandon 1: Change is an illusion (Parmenides, Zeno, Eleatics).

Abandon 2: Matter (indeed *everything*) changes (Heracleitus).

Abandon 3: Matter and the world are not all there is; there is also the void—and the changing configurations of matter within it (atomism).

Taking up the third course, let us continue to follow the atomistic route. Note that this does not *just* call for abandoning 3, but also calls for sophisticating 2 to the following:

2'. Matter as such is *not* changeable—it only changes in point of its variable rearrangements.

The distinction between *positional* changes and *compositional* changes comes to the fore here. This line of development has recourse to a "saving distinction" by introducing the new topic of variable configurations (as contrasted with such necessary and invariable states as the shapes of the atoms themselves).

To be sure, matters do not end here. A new cycle of inconsistency looms ahead. For this new topic paves the way for the following apory:

III

1. All possibilities of variation are actually realized.

2. Various different world arrangements are possible.

3. Only one world is real.

Again different resolutions are obviously available here:

Reject 1: A theory of real chance (*tuchê*) or contingency that sees various possibilities as going unrealized (Empedocles).

Reject 2: A doctrine of universal necessitation (the "block universe" of Parmenides).

Reject 3: A theory of many worlds (Democritus and atomism in general).

As the atomistic resolution represented by the second course was developed, apory broken out again:

IV

1. Matter as such never changes—the only change it admits are its rearrangements.
2. The nature of matter is indifferent to change. Its rearrangements are contingent and potentially variable.
3. Its changes of condition are inherent in the (unchanging) nature of matter—they are necessary, not contingent.

Here the orthodox atomistic solution would lie in abandoning 3 and replacing it with the following:

3'. Its changes of condition are not necessitated by the nature of matter. They are indeed quasi-necessitated by being law determined, but law is something independent of the nature of matter.

The distinction between internally necessitated changes and externally and accidentally imposed ones enters upon the scene. This resolution introduces a new theme—namely, *law determination* (as introduced by the Stoics).

Yet when one seeks to apply this idea it seems plausible to add:

V

4. Certain material changes (contingencies, concomitant with free human actions) are not law determined.

Apory now breaks out once more; the need for an exit from incon-sistency again arises. And such an exit was afforded by abandoning 4, as with the law abrogation envisaged in the notorious "swerve" of Epicurus, or by abandoning 3', as with the more rigoristic atomism of Lucretius.

The developmental sequence from I through V represents an evolution of philosophical reflection through successive layers of aporetic inconsistency, duly separated from one another by succes-sive distinctions. This process led from the crude doctrines of Ionian theorists to the vastly more elaborate and sophisticated doctrines of later Greek atomism.

This historical illustration also indicates an important general principle. The continual introduction of the new ideas that arise in the wake of new distinctions means that the ground of philosophy is always shifting beneath our feet. And it is through distinctions that philosophy's prime mode of innovation—namely *conceptual* innova-tion—comes into play. And those novel distinctions for our concepts and contexts for our theses alter the very substance of the old theses. The dialectical exchange of objection and response constantly moves the discussion onto new—and increasingly sophisticated—ground. The resolution of antinomies through new distinctions is thus a matter of creative innovation whose outcome cannot be foreseen.

►9◄

The Rationale of Aporetic Variation

The definitive task of aporetics is consistency restoration. Confronted with an inconsistent set of otherwise plausible propositions in any context of deliberation, it is only sensible to seek to maintain rational consistency. Something has to give way in the interests of coherence. And in general the reasonable approach here is to employ situationally appropriate right-of-way considerations to break the chain of inconsistency at its weakest link(s). And this sort of problem arises in a wide variety of cognitive situations—rational inquiry not least among them.

With regard to the standards of precedence and priority for apory resolution, there are three distinctively different lines of approach:

Thesis plausibility: The guide to priority is evidentiation—that is, thesis security in point of supportive grounding pivots on conformity with experience.

Informativeness: The guide to priority is informativeness in answering questions. Explanatory power becomes the determinative factor, so that generality and fundamentality come to the fore.

Systematist: The guide to priority is coherentist philosophizing. This approach seeks the coordinated balance of a productive tension between the competing factors of security and informativeness.

This overall situation is linked to a very fundamental principle of epistemology: There is in general an inverse relationship between the precision or definiteness of a judgment and its security; detail and probability stand in a competing relationship. Increased confidence in the correctness of our estimates can always be purchased at the price of decreased accuracy. We estimate the height of the tree at *around* 25 feet. We are *quite sure* that the tree is 25±5 feet high. We are *virtually certain* that its height is 25±10 feet. But we can be *completely and absolutely sure* that its height is between 1 inch and 100 yards. Of this we can be "completely sure" in the sense that we are "absolutely certain," "certain beyond the shadow of a doubt," "as certain as we can be of anything in the world," "so sure that we would be willing to stake our life on it," and the like. For any sort of estimate whatsoever there is always a characteristic trade-off relationship between the evidential *security* of the estimate, on the one hand (as determinable on the basis of its probability or degree of acceptability), and, on the other hand, its contentual *definitiveness* (exactness, detail, precision, etc.). A situation of the sort depicted by the curve of display 9.1 obtains with the result that a *complementarity* relationship of sorts obtains here as between definiteness and security.[1]

And there is much to be said for taking this line. After all, we want answers to our questions, but we want these answers to make up a coherent systematic whole. It is neither just answers (regardless of their substantiation) nor just safe claims (regardless of their lack of informativeness) we want but a reasonable mix of the two—a judicious balance that systematizes our commitments in a functionally effective way.

The Rationale of Aporetic Variation

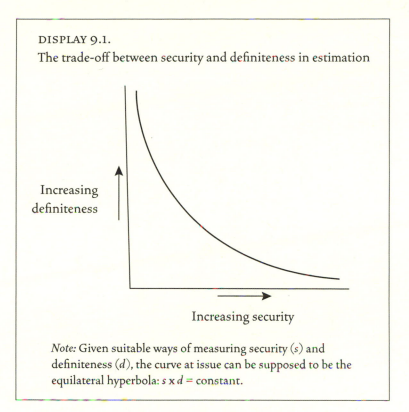

DISPLAY 9.1.

The trade-off between security and definiteness in estimation

Increasing
definiteness

Increasing security

Note: Given suitable ways of measuring security (s) and definiteness (d), the curve at issue can be supposed to be the equilateral hyperbola: $s \times d$ = constant.

Overall, however, the business of weakest-link determination functions rather differently in different areas of inquiry. And it does so in alignment with the particular purposive nature of the context of thought that is at issue. For the frailty at issue is contextually variable. Different cognitive enterprises have different aims and objectives in view, and this circumstance will control what is at issue with assertoric strength and weakness. The overall situation is surveyed in display 9.2. Thus, for example, the situation in systematist philosophizing is accordingly neither one of pure speculation, where informativeness alone governs conflict resolution, nor one of scientific/inductive inquiry, where evidential coherence governs this process, but a judicious combination of the two.

Variant versions of the weakest-link principle and their rationale

When an inconsistency in the wake of beliefs arises in the setting of	And this happens in the wake of	Then the weakest link will be	Because in this particular context we prioritize the value of
Empirical inquiry	New discoveries	The most weakly evidentiated	Security
Thought experimentation	Thought-experimental assumptions	The systemically least deeply entrenched	Informativeness
Counterfactual speculation	Belief-contravening suppositions (systemically least central)	The contextually least fundamental	Overall comprehensibility
Counterfactual history	Counterfactual speculation	The most radical depiction for established norms	Overall coherence
Paradoxes	Conflicting plausible contentions	The least inherently plausible	Security
Empiricist philosophy	Data accumulation	The least consonant with the fundamental commitments of one's overall position	Overall credibility
Speculative philosophy	Explanatory conjectures	The least informative	Explanatory fertility
Systemic philosophy	Synoptic deliberation	The least smoothly fitting	Systemic unity

And so, while in every sort of aporetic situation we confront the same basic issue of using right-of-way priority considerations to eliminate the aporetic conflict and restore inconsistency, the process proceeds quite differently in different contexts designed in each case to fit the purposive needs of the situation. For this difference in approach is grounded in the characteristic teleology of the domain—in the functionality of purpose that defines the goal structure of the particular cognitive realm at issue. The aims of the enterprise and the varying sources of inconsistency-involvement conspire to make for different approaches to consistency resolution in different aporetic contexts. Thus empirical inquiry prioritizes security, while speculative philosophy prioritizes systematicity in seeking a deeper understanding of the big issues. We do not just want answers, we want *systemically cogent* answers that have the backing of good reasons and answers that harmonize with the others that we offer in different context. Systematization alone is the proper instrument of this domain. Our norms and standards here will have to be articulated in terms of an optimal cognitive harmonization—of conformity to the fundamental commitments at which one arrives on the basis of the general course of one's experience.[2]

How all this works out is indicated in display 9.3. As the tabulation shows, there are basically three modes of aporetic inquiry. One is the *security-intensive* (evidentiation having priority 1; informativeness having priority 4). Yet another is the *information-intensive* (evidentiation having priority 4 or 5; informativeness having priority 1 or 2). And the third mode is that of the *midrange balance*, which characterizes a certain particularly cautious sort of coherentist philosophical inquiry.

After all, security and evidentiation alone does not always carry the day. Informativeness also matters. Man is a rational animal, schooled by evolution to an economy of effect—intellectual as well as physical. And so in factual inquiry, rational economy and purposive efficacy are our guiding stars and provide the key to the principles of

DISPLAY 9.3.						
A comparison of standards for prioritization in consistency restoration						
			Contextual priority ranking			
	Empirical		History		Philosophy	
Support Status of a Thesis	Inquiry	Counter-factuals	Paradoxes	Speculative	Empirical	Speculative
Evidentiation/ security/ specificity	1	5	1	2	1	4
Internal plausibility	2	4	2	3	2	3
Nomic fun-damentality/ theoretical elegance/ harmony	3	3	3	5	3	2
Informative-ness/ generality/ systematicity	4	2	4	5	4	1
Postulation/ supposition	–	1	–	1	–	–

plausibility and presumption on which our cognitive proceedings are based. However, matters stand very differently in the context of science and the everyday affairs of life. In science we demand accuracy and precision, while in ordinary life it is reliability that comes to the forefront. And insofar as our ignorance of relevant matters leads us to be vague in our judgments, we may well manage to enhance the likelihood of being right. The fact of the matter is that we have this ironic principle: By constraining us to make vaguer judgments, ignorance enhances our access to correct information (albeit at the cost of less detail and precision). Thus, if I have forgotten that Seattle

The Rationale of Aporetic Variation

is in Washington State and I am forced to guess where it is, then I might well erroneously locate it in Oregon. Nevertheless, my vague judgment that "Seattle is located in the northwestern United States" is quite correct. This state of affairs means that when the truth of our claims is critical, we generally play it safe and make our commitments less definite and detailed. And so in ordinary life we prioritize security over informativeness. In speculative philosophizing, on the other hand, one does the very reverse.

All in all, then, the rationale for a particular mode of prioritization lies in the specific goal and purpose of the domain of deliberations at issue. Just this essentially pragmatic consideration must be allowed to determine the correlative principle of prioritization.

As these considerations indicate, the goals and purposes will in the end prove to be determinative for our modus operandi with consistency restoration in different areas of rational inquiry. The overall goal structure of the realm of deliberation will determine the appropriate standard of precedence in resolving right-of-way issues in cognitive conflicts. The upshot is clear: while the same fundamental aporetic goal of consistency maintenance prevails throughout all these variant situations, the proper ways and means by which this is to be accomplished will be detailed by the epistemic objectives that characterize the particular situation at hand. Thus here, as elsewhere, the proper manner of proceeding is geared to the specific context of relevant purpose. And so, even in theoretical matters the pragmatic dimension is bound to come to the fore.

NOTES

CHAPTER 1: *The Nature of Apories*

1. The terminology is adapted from the Greek *aporetikê technê*, the "aporetic art" of articulating, analyzing, and resolving *aporia*, or paradoxes. The conception of such an enterprise as central to philosophy figured prominently in the work of German philosopher Nicolai Hartmann (1882–1950). See his *Grundzüge einer Metaphysik der Erkenntnis*, 5th ed. (Berlin: W. de Gruyter, 1965).

2. Blaise Pascal, *Penseés*, No. 791, 566th ed. (New York: Modern Library), 185. Recall the dictum that "consistency is the bugaboo of small minds."

3. For Protagoras, see Zeller, *Philosophie der Griechen*, vols. 1–2, 6th ed. (Leipzig: Rersland, 1929), 1296–1304. See also Plato's dialogues *Protagoras* and *The Sophist*. Protagoras was perfectly prepared to accept the paradoxical consequence that this holds also for the very thesis at issue.

4. "Protagoras ait, de omnis re in utrumque partem disputari posse ex aequo, et de hac ipsa, an ominis res in utrumque partem disputabilis sit" (Seneca, *Epistola moralia*, 14:88, 43).

5. Compare Nicholas Rescher and Robert Brandom, *The Logic of Inconsistency* (Oxford: Blackwell, 1979).

CHAPTER 2: *Coherentism*

1. Already Heracleitus maintained the reality of conflicts and contradictions in nature. Cf. Diels-Kranz, *Fragments der Vorsolersatikes* (Balsun: Wer-

demergh, 1952), §22, B10, B49a, B51, etc. He taught that opposites really do characterize the same subject. Sextus Empiricus wrote, "Anesidemus and his followers used to say that the Sceptic Way is a road leading up to the Heraclitean philosophy, since to hold [with the Sceptics] that the same thing is the subject of opposite appearances is a preliminary to holding [with the Heracliteans] that it is the subject of opposite realities" (*Outlines of Pyrrhonism*, 1:210 [cf. n. 63], and compare Aristotle, *Metaphysics*, 12a24ff.).

The sceptics held to the omni-indeterminacy thesis that one can never assert the truth either of *p* or of ~*p*; one can sometimes assert the truth both of *p* and of ~*p*. Even as the reality-is-contradiction-free school can trace its ancestry to Parmenides, so the reality-incorporates-contradictions school can claim the paternity of Heracleitus.

2. See Hegel, *Science of Logic*, n. §67. But contrast McTaggart's interpretation in *Studies in the Hegelian Dialectic*, 3 vols. (Cambridge: Cambridge University Press, 1922), §8. Hegel's opponents also maintained the realization of contradictions in the world. See Kierkegaard, *Concluding Unscientific Postscript*, 510–11, and *Philosophical Fragments*, chap. 3.

3. D. C. Makinson, "The Paradox of the Preface," *Analysis* 25 (1964): 205–7. Compare H. E. Kyburg Jr., "Conjunctivitis," in *Induction, Acceptance, and Rational Belief*, ed. M. Swain (Dordrecht: D. Reidel, 1970), 55–82, see esp. 77; and also R. M. Chisholm, *The Theory of Knowledge*, 2nd ed. (Englewood Cliffs, NJ: Prentice Hall, 1976), 96–97. The fundamental idea of the Preface Paradox goes back to C. S. Peirce, who wrote that "while holding certain propositions to be each individually perfectly certain, we may and ought to think it likely that some of them, if not more, are false" (*Collected Papers*, vol. 5 [Cambridge, MA: Harvard University Press, 1934], sec. 5, p. 498.)

4. Keith Lehrer, *Knowledge* (Oxford: Clarendon Press, 1974), 203.

5. Ibid.

6. René Descartes, *Meditations on First Philosophy*, no. 1, trans. R. M. Eaton.

7. The defeat of a defeasible presumption relates (in the case of a specific presumption of fact) to its upset by falsification in a particular instance rather than the distinction of the presumption rule as such. Of course, such a general rule or principle—the presumptive veracity of a reliable source, for example— can also be *invalidated* ("falsified" would be inappropriate). For a further discussion of the relevant issues, see Nicholas Rescher, *Methodological Pragmatism* (Oxford: Basil Blackwell, 1976).

8. Consideration of the rule of presumption in logic and the theory of knowledge goes back to Richard Whately, *Elements of Rhetoric* (London and Oxford: Oxford University Press, 1928). The theme was reintroduced into the contemporary scene in Nicholas Rescher, *Dialectics* (Albany: SUNY Press, 1972). See also E. Ullman-Margalit, "On Presumption," *Journal of Philosophy* 80 (1983): 143–63; and Douglas N. Walton, *Argumentation Scheme for Presumptive Reasoning* (Mahwark, NJ: Laurence Erlbaum Associates, 1996).

9. All this, of course, does not deal with the question of the tile status of this rule itself and of the nature of its own justification. It is important in the present context to stress the *regulative* role of plausibilistic considerations. This now becomes a matter of *epistemic policy* ("Give priority to contentions which treat like cases alike") and not a metaphysically laden contention regarding the ontology of nature (as with the—blatantly false—descriptive claim "Nature is uniform"). The plausibilistic theory of inductive reasoning sees uniformity as a *regulative principle of epistemic policy* in grounding our choices, not as a *constitutive principle* of ontology. As a "regulative principle of epistemic policy" its status is *methodological*—and thus its justification is in the final analysis pragmatic. See the author's *Methodological Pragmatism* (Oxford: Basil Blackwell, 1976).

10. See Ferdinand Gonseth, "La notion du normal," *Dialectica* 3 (1947): 243–52, as well as Nicholas Rescher, *Philosophical Standardism* (Pittsburgh: University of Pittsburgh Press, 1994).

11. For a closer study of the notion of plausibility and its function in rational deliberation, see Nicholas Rescher, *Plausible Reasoning* (Assen: Van Gorcum, 1976), and *Presumption and the Practices of Tentative Cognition* (Cambridge: Cambridge University Press, 2006).

12. Some of the key ideas of this chapter trace back to the author's *The Coherence Theory of Truth* (Oxford: Clarendon Press, 1973).

CHAPTER 3: *Counterfactual Conditionals*

1. Herodotus, *History*, 2.20: 2–3. For more information on the historical background of counterfactuals, see the author's "Thought Experimentation in Presocratic Philosophy," in *Thought Experiments in Science and Philosophy*, ed. Tamara Horowitz and Gerald J. Massey (Lanham, MD: Rowman & Littlefield, 1991), 31–41.

2. The pioneer studies are R. M. Chisholm, "The Contrary-to-Fact Conditional," *Mind* 55 (1946): 289–307, and Nelson Goodman, "The Problem of

Counterfactual Conditionals," *Journal of Philosophy* 44 (1947): 113–28. See also E. F. Schneider, "Recent Discussions of Subjunctive Conditionals," *Review of Metaphysics* 6 (1952): 623–47.

3. See the excellent and informative survey by N. J. Roese and J. M. Olsen, "Self-Esteem and Counterfactual Thinking," *Journal of Personality and Social Psychology* 65 (1993): 199–206.

4. The pioneer studies are Chisholm, "The Contrary-to-Fact Conditional," and Goodman, "The Problem of Counterfactual Conditionals." Schneider's "Recent Discussions of Subjunctive Conditionals" gives a helpful survey of the early literature.

5. Sometimes what looks like a counterfactual conditional is only so in appearance. Thus consider "If Napoleon and Alexander the Great were fused into a single individual, what a great general that would be!" What is at issue here is not really a counterfactual based on the weird hypothesis of a fusion of two people into one. Rather, what we have is merely a rhetorically striking reformulation of the truism that "Anyone who combines the military talents of Napoleon and of Alexander is certainly a great general."

6. The Stalnaker-Lewis theory of counterfactuals that is nowadays favored among possible-world semanticists is predicated on the idea of a metric of distance between worlds measurable by assessing their similarity. This supposition is open to the fatal objection that there is no absolute concept of similarity at all, seeing that all similarity is a matter of respect and that we have no categorical way of weighing different respects against one another in some issue-neutral way.

7. Note that the claim "If Hamlet had actually existed, he could not have been a more complex personality than the protagonist of Shakespeare's play" is effectively tantamount to "The protagonist of Shakespeare's *Hamlet* is depicted as having an endlessly complex personality."

8. The treatment of suppositions presented in this chapter was initially set out in the author's "Belief-Contravening Suppositions," *Philosophical Review* 87 (1961): 176–96, and subsequently developed in Rescher, *Hypothetical Reasoning* (Amsterdam: North Holland, 1964).

9. S. O. Hansson, "The Emperor's New Clothes: Some Recurring Problems in the Formal Analysis of Counterfactual," in *Conditionals: From Philosophy to Computer Science*, ed. G. Crocco, L. F. Fariñas de Cerro, and A. Herzig (Oxford: Clarendon Press, 1995), 15–17.

10. On this issue, see Rescher, *Hypothetical Reasoning*, and Isaac Levi, *For the*

Sake of Argument (Cambridge: Cambridge University Press, 1996). The sort of logical or quasi-logical approach envisioned by various 1940s theorists such as Chisholm, "The Contrary-to-Fact Conditional," and Goodman, "The Problem of Counterfactual Conditionals," is foredoomed to failure, as the subsequent unfolding of discussion during the second half of the twentieth century has made only too clear.

11. This point was stressed in Rescher, *Hypothetical Reasoning*. It has also been argued in Hansson, "The Emperor's New Clothes."

12. See Hansson, "The Emperor's New Clothes," 15–17.

13. Compare R. M. Chisholm, "Law Statements and Counterfactual Inference," *Analysis* 15 (1955): 102–5.

14. See Goodman, "The Problem of Counterfactual Conditionals."

15. See David K. Lewis, *Counterfactuals* (Cambridge, MA: Harvard University Press, 1973), 3.

16. See W.V. O. Quine, "On What There Is," *Review of Metaphysics* 2 (1948): 23.

17. For further aspects of the present line of approach to counterfactual analysis, see Rescher, *Conditionals* (Cambridge, MA: MIT Press, 2007).

18. This is a point the author has argued for many years. See his "Belief-Contravening Suppositions," *Philosophical Review* 70 (1961): 176–96, as well as *Hypothetical Reasoning* (Amsterdam: North Holland, 1964) and *Conceptual Idealism* (Oxford: Basil Blackwell, 1973). For supporting evidence, see M. D. Braine and D. F. O'Brian, "A Theory of If," *Psychological Review* 98 (1991): 182–203, and N. J. Roese and James M. Olson, *What Might Have Been: The Social Psychology of Counterfactual Thinking* (Mahwah, NJ: Erlbaum, 1995), 3–4.

CHAPTER 4: *Variant Analyses of Counterfactuals and Problems of Probability*

1. F. P. Ramsey, "Law and Causality," in *Foundation Essays in Philosophy, Logic, Mathematics and Economics*, ed. D. H. Mellor (London: Routledge & Kegan Paul, 1978). See also Nils-Eric Sahlin, *The Philosophy of F. P. Ramsey* (Cambridge: Cambridge University Press, 1990), 121.

2. W. L. Harper, G. A. Pearce, and R. Stalnaker, eds., *Ifs: Conditionals, Beliefs, Decision, Chance, and Time*, The Western Ontario Series in Philosophy of Science (Dordrecht: D. Reidel, 1981), 4.

3. Robert C. Stalnaker, "A Theory of Conditionals," *Studies in Logical Theory*, American Philosophical Quarterly Monograph Series, No. 2, p. 100.

4. See André Fuhrmann and Isaac Levi, "Undercutting the Ramsey Test

for Conditionals," in *The Logic of Strategy*, ed. Christina Biccieri et al. (Oxford: Oxford University Press, 1999). However, these authors avert the difficulties they encounter by introducing so complex a variant of the "Inductive Ramsey Test" that the effect is one of employing a steamroller to crack a nut. A theoretical analysis of counterfactuals must not lose sight of the fact that they are a commonplace resource of ordinary discourse. A theory not attuned to commonsensical considerations cannot meet the needs of the situation.

5. W. B. Mendelson, "Clinical Distinctions between Long-Acting and Short-Acting Benzodiazepines," *Clinical Journal of Psychiatry* 53 (December 1992): 4–7.

6. Robert C. Stalnaker, "A Theory of Conditionals," *Studies in Logical Theory*, American Philosophical Quarterly Monograph Series, No. 2 (Oxford: Blackwell, 1968), 103–4.

7. The idea of differentially "far-out" suppositions undoubtedly plays a role in the psychology of speculation. (See Daniel Kahneman and D. T. Miller, "Norm Theory: Comparing Reality to Its Alternatives," *Psychological Review* 93 [1986]: 136–53.) But this is always a matter of specific context, and its across-the-board generalization over "possible worlds" is open to question.

8. The theoretical basis of possible-world avoidance is set out in considerable detail in Nicholas Rescher, *Imagining Irreality* (Chicago: Carus Publishing, 2003).

9. Ibid.

10. On these issues, see Nicholas Rescher, "The Fallacy of Respect Neglect," *Philosophy and Phenomenological Research* 71 (2005): 392–98.

11. See Harper, Pearce, and Stalnaker, *Ifs: Conditionals, Beliefs, Decision, Chance, and Time*, 9.

12. On this issue, compare also Kit Fine, "Review of Lewis's *Counterfactual*," *Mind* 84 (1975): 451–58.

13. See David K. Lewis, "Counterfactual Dependence and Time's Arrow," *Nous* 13 (1979): 57–91. Lewis speaks of these fictions as matters of "weights or priorities." But these are very different matters, since weighing counterfactuals envisions a blending of compound considerations, while prioritization looks to a lexical ordering. Lewis's account has other internal difficulties as well. (See Adam Elga, "Statistical Mechanics and the Asymmetry of Counterfactual Dependence," *Philosophy of Science* [Supplementary Volume PSA 2000] [Bloomington, IN: Philosophy of Science Association, 2002].)

14. This is an oversimplification. On Lewis's approach, we would need to construct a possible world to implement the scenario at issue—a task that could be achieved in theory in endlessly different ways and in practice in none.

15. See Nicholas Rescher, "Belief-Contravening Suppositions," *Philosophical Review* 87 (1961): 176–96, and Rescher, *Hypothetical Reasoning*.

16. On these issues, see Rescher, *Imagining Irreality*.

17. Igal Kvart, *A Theory of Counterfactuals* (Indianapolis: Hacket, 1986), xiii.

18. See Fabrizio Mondadori and Adam Martin, "Modal Realism: The Poisoned Pawn," *Philosophical Review* 85 (1976): 3–20.

19. Lycan, *Real Conditionals*, 17.

20. On these issues, see Rescher, *Conditionals*. The basic point of divergence at issue here was already articulated by David Lewis. He wrote: "Rescher's *Hypothetical Reasoning* is an approach . . . [that is] principally concerned with [epistemic] conditions of assertability or acceptability for counterfactuals, rather than with [ontological] truth conditions" (Lewis, *Counterfactuals*, 70).

And again in discussing Pollock's *Subjunctive Reasoning,* Kvart wrote: "His [Pollock's] basic strategy, . . . reminiscent of Rescher's in his *Hypothetical Reasoning* (Amsterdam: North Holland, 1964) . . . seems to rest the analysis of counterfactuals on epistemological foundations, a move quite different from the ontological orientation discussed above" (Kvart, *A Theory of Counterfactuals*, 191). This observation too is right on the money. Unlike all of the subsequently fashionable possible-world approaches (Stalnaker, Lewis, etc.), my own approach proceeds on the basis of fundamentally epistemological considerations—and in doing so lays some claims to addressing the task of explaining how counterfactuals actually work in discourse by inherently more natural and unproblematic means. On the difficulty of recounting the possible world treatment of candidates with the commemorative realities of conditional discourses, see Braine and O'Brian, "A Theory of *If*," 182–203.

21. See Ernest W. Adams, "Probability and the Logic of Conditionals," in *Aspects of Inductive Logic,* ed. J. Hintikka and P. Suppes (Amsterdam: North-Holland, 1966), 256–316, and idem, *The Logic of Conditionals: An Application of Probability to Deductive Logic* (Dordrecht: D. Reidel, 1975); David H. Sanford, *If P, Then Q: Conditionals and the Foundations of Reasoning* (London: Routledge, 1989); and in particular the critique of this approach in David K. Lewis, "Prob-

abilities of Conditionals and Conditional Probabilities," *Philosophical Review* 85 (1976): 297–315, 581–89.

22. On viable conditionals with impossible antecedents, see Lewis, *Counterfactuals*, 24–26. After briefly toying with the idea of impossible possible worlds, Lewis proposes to regard such counterfactuals as uniformly "vacuously true," an approach that would saddle us with all sorts of bizarre counterfactuals that no one would want to assert.

CHAPTER 5: *The Aporetics of Counterfactual History*

1. When British Prime Minister Lord Rosebery was installed as Lord Rector of Glasgow University in the late 1800s, he gave a widely reported inaugural address in which he stated that if the American Revolution had been averted there would have resulted "a self-adjusting system of representation and in due time, when the majority of seats in the Imperial Parliament should belong to the section beyond the seas, the seat of empire would have been moved solemnly across the Atlantic."

2. Problematic or not, this sort of thing has—rather surprisingly—become increasingly popular among historians in recent days. See Robert Cowley, ed., *What If* (New York: G. P. Putnam's Sons, 1998) and Niall Ferguson, ed., *Virtual History* (New York: Basic Books, 1999). Greenhill Books of London has launched an entire series along these lines: Kenneth Macksey, ed., *The Hitler Options: Alternate Decisions of World War II* (1998); idem, *Invasions: The Alternate History of the German Invasion of England, July 1940* (1999); Robert Sobel, *For Want of a Nail: If Burgoyne Had Won at Saratoga* (1997); Peter Tsouras, *Disaster at D-Day: The Germans Defeat the Allies, June 1944* (2000); Peter Tsouras, *Gettysburg: An Alternate History* (1997); Brian Thomsen and Martin H. Greenberg, eds., *Alternate Gettysburgs* (New York: Berkeley Books, 2002). The June 2004 issue of the *American Historical Review* contains a "Focus Essay" by Martin Bunze entitled "Counterfactual History: A User's Guide," accompanied by an open invitation to participate in an outcome discussion of the topic. Also worth noting is Nelson Polsby, *What If? Essays in Social Science Fiction* (Lexington, MA: Lewis Publishing, 1982).

3. See Lewis, "Counterfactual Dependence and Time's Arrow"; Jonathan Bennett, "Counterfactuals and Temporal Direction," *Philosophical Review* 93 (1984): 57–91.

1. For a fuller treatment of this issue, see Nicholas Rescher, "Ueber einen zentralen unterschied zwishen theorie und Praxis," *Deutsche zeitschrift fuer philosophie* 47 (1999): 171–82.

2. Diogenes Laertius, *Lives of Eminent Philosophers*, 2:111, 4:39, reports that some think that this sophism is a joke aimed at the cuckold.

3. On the various ancient discussions of *The Paradox of the Horns*, see Prantl, *Geschichte*, 1:53. The paradox is almost as bizarre as the sophistical *Dog Paradox* that turns on the reasoning:

That dog is your dog.

That dog is a father.

Therefore: That dog is your father.

This paradox preoccupied the Megarian paradox theorists and also the Sophists (see Plato, *Euthydemus*, 299E). (Some elaborated the sophism by adding: "You beat that dog. Therefore: You beat your father.") Another variant of such a paradox was discussed by the Stoics: "He is a bad person; he is a butcher; therefore, he is a bad butcher." (See Prantl, *Geschichte*, 1:492.)

4. For the relevant issues at the level of decision theory in general, see R. D. Luce and H. Raiffa, *Games and Decisions* (New York: Wiley, 1957).

5. See chapter 5 of his *Autobiography*.

6. On this paradox and related issues, see Richard M. Gale, *The Nature and Existence of God* (Cambridge: Cambridge University Press, 1991).

7. To be sure, a committed atheist would have a very different priority ranking—one in which (1) would presumably be the low man on the totem pole.

8. Some concrete illustrations will be given later.

9. The distinctions at issue here go back to Husserl's distinction between the hermeneutically and the informatively meaningless, between non-sense (*Unsinn*) and contra-sense (*Widersinn*). The former is radically meaningless; the latter simply confused and self-conflicted. See Edmund Husserl, *Logische Untersuchungen*, trans. J. N. Findlay (New York: Humanities Press, 1970), 1:110–16.

10. The paradox was discussed by G. E. Moore in his book *Ethics* (Oxford: Clarendon Press, 1912) and also in P. Schilpp, *The Philosophy of G. E. Moore* (Chicago: Open Court, 1942), 430–33, and in P. Schilpp, ed., *The Philosophy of Bertrand Russell* (Chicago: Open Court, 1944), 204. (The former of these books contains an article on Moore's Paradox by Morris Lazerowitz [371–93].) The

paradox was already known in medieval times. Already Albert of Saxony discussed the paradoxical nature of propositions of the form "Socrates believes himself deceived in believing a certain proposition A," seeing that in believing A Socrates maintains it as true, and in believing himself deceived he rejects it as false. On this basis, Albert developed a complex argument to the effect that it is impossible for Socrates (i.e., anyone) to know that he is mistaken about a concrete matter of fact (363–64). And analogously, William of Heytesbury (ca. 1310–ca. 1370) argued in his *Regulae solvendi sophismata* (ca. 1335) that a person cannot doubt something he knows. *Nihil scire potest nisi verum* became an accepted dictum.

11. Think of Spinoza's scornful dismissal of "one who says that he has a true idea and yet doubts whether it may not be false" (*Ethics*, Bk. I, prop. 8, sect. 2).

12. Issues relevant to this chapter's deliberations are also addressed in Nicholas Rescher, *Paradoxes* (Chicago: Open Court, 2001).

CHAPTER 7: *Philosophical Aporetics*

1. Kant wrote: "Now *wonder* is a shock of the moral sense, arising from the incompatibility of a representation . . . with the principles already lying at its basis, which provokes a doubt as to whether we have rightly seen or rightly judged" (*Critique of Judgment*, trans. J. H. Bernard [London: Macmillan, 1892], 211). Our present construction of the term generalizes this overly narrow construction to include a conflict of "beliefs" as well as one of "representations."

2. Spinoza, *Ethics*, Book I, prop. 33, scholium 2.

3. *Omnis negatio est determinatio*. Abraham Wolf, ed. and trans., *The Correspondence of Spinoza* (London: Allan and Unwin, 1928), letter no. 59.

4. The conception of plausibility (and, in particular its difference from the more familiar conception of *probability*) is explained in the author's book on *Plausible Reasoning* (Assen: Van Gorcum, 1976).

5. Friedrich Nietzsche, *The Genealogy of Morals*, Pt. II, sect. xv.

6. For further details, see Rescher, *Hypothetical Reasoning*.

7. This general position that philosophical problems involve antinomic situations from which there are only finitely many exits (which, in general, the historical course of philosophical development actually indicates) is foreshadowed in the deliberations of Wilhelm Dilthey. See his *Gesammelte Schriften* (Stuttgart and Göttingen: Teubner and Vandenhoeck & Ruprecht, 1961), 8:138.

8. Issues relevant to this chapter's deliberations are also addressed in Rescher, *The Strife of Systems*. The book is also available in Spanish, Italian, and German translations.

CHAPTER 8: *The Dialectics of Philosophical Development*

1. Frank P. Ramsey, *The Foundations of Mathematics and Other Logical Essays*, ed. R. B. Braithwaite (London: K. Paul, Trench, Trubner & Co., 1931), 115–16.

CHAPTER 9: *The Rationale of Aporetic Variation*

1. This circumstance did not elude Neils Bohr himself, the father of complementarity theory in physics. In later years, Bohr emphasized the importance of complementarity for matters far removed from physics. There is a story that Bohr was once asked in German, "What is the quality that is complementary to truth (*Wahrheit*)?" After some thought, he answered, "Clarity" (*Klarheit*) (Stephen Weinberg, *Dreams of a Final Theory* [New York: Pantheon Books, 1992], 74n10.)

2. On this theme, see the Nicholas Rescher, *Cognitive Harmony* (Pittsburgh: University of Pittsburgh Press, 2005).

BIBLIOGRAPHY

Adams, Ernest W. *The Logic of Conditionals: An Application of Probability to De-*
   ductive Logic. Dordrecht: D. Reidel, 1975.

———. "Probability and the Logic of Conditionals." In *Aspects of Inductive*
   Logic, ed. J. Hintikka and P. Suppes, 256–316. Amsterdam: North-Holland,
   1966.

Aristotle. *Metaphysics.*

Bennett, Jonathan. "Counterfactuals and Temporal Direction." *Philosophical*
   Review 93 (1984): 57–91.

———. *A Philosophical Guide to Conditionals.* Oxford: Clarendon Press, 2003.

Braun, Lucien. *L'histoire de l'histoire de la philosophie.* Paris: Ophrys, 1973.

Bunze, Martin. "Counterfactual History: A User's Guide." *American Historical*
   Review (2004): 57–91.

Chisholm, R. M. "The Contrary-to-Fact Conditional." *Mind* 55 (1946):
   289–307.

———. "Law Statements and Counterfactual Inference." *Analysis* 15 (1955):
   97–105.

———. *The Theory of Knowledge.* 2nd ed. Englewood Cliffs, NJ: Prentice-Hall,
   1977.

Collins, John David, Edward J. Hall, and L. A. Paul. *Causation and Counterfac-*
   tuals. Cambridge, Mass.: MIT Press, 2004.

Cowley, Robert, ed. *What If.* New York: G. P. Putnam's Sons, 1998.

Dilthey, Wilhelm. *Gesammelte Schriften.* Vol. 8. Stuttgart and Göttingen: Teubner and Vandenhoeck & Ruprecht, 1961.

Elga, Adam. "Statistical Mechanics and the Asymmetry of Counterfactual Dependence." *Philosophy of Science* (Supplementary Volume PSA 2000). Bloomington, IN: Philosophy of Science Association, 2002.

Ferguson, Niall, ed. *Virtual History.* New York: Basic Books, 1999.

Fine, Kit. "Review of Lewis's *Counterfactual.*" *Mind* 84 (1975): 451–58.

Fuhrmann, André, and Isaac Levi. "Undercutting the Ramsey Test for Conditionals." In *The Logic of Strategy*, ed. Christina Biccieri, Richard Jeffrey, and Brian Skyrms. Oxford: Oxford University Press, 1999.

Gadamer, Hans-Georg. *Die Begriffsgeschichte und der Sprache der Philosophie.* Opladen: Westdeutscher Verlag, 1971.

Gonseth, Ferdinand. "La notion du normal." *Dialectica* 3 (1947): 243–52.

Goodman, Nelson. *Fact, Fiction, and Forecast.* Cambridge, MA: Harvard University Press, 1983.

———. "The Problem of Counterfactual Conditionals." *Journal of Philosophy* 44 (1947): 113–28.

Graf, Gerhard. *Die sokratische Aporie im Denken Platons.* Winterthur: P. G. Keller, 1963.

Halper, E. "The Origin of Aristotle's Metaphysical *Aporiai.*" *Apeiron* 21 (1988): 1–27.

Hansson, S. O. "The Emperor's New Clothes: Some Recurring Problems in the Formal Analysis of Counterfactual." In *Conditionals: From Philosophy to Computer Science*, ed. G. Crocco, L. F. Fariñas de Cerro, and A. Herzig. Oxford: Clarendon Press, 1995.

Harper, William L. "A Sketch of Some Recent Developments in the Theory of Conditionals." In *Ifs: Conditionals, Beliefs, Decision, Chance, and Time*, ed. W. L. Harper, G. A. Pearce, and R. Stalnaker. The Western Ontario Series in Philosophy of Science. Dordrecht: D. Reidel, 1981.

Hartmann, Nicolai. *Grundzüge einer Metaphysik der Erkenntnis.* 5th ed. Berlin: W. de Gruyter, 1965.

———. *Systematische Philosophie.* Stuttgart and Berlin: Kohlhammer, 1942.

Hegel, Georg Wilhelm Friedrich. *Philosophy of History.*

———. *Science of Logic.*

Herodotus. *History*, 2.20: 2–3.

Husserl, Edmund. *Logische Untersuchungen.* 2 vols. Halle: M. Niemeyer, 1900–1901.

Ilting, Karl-Heinz. "Aporie." In *Handbuch philosophischer Grundbegriffe*, vol. 1., ed. Hermann Krings, Hans Michael Baumgartner, and Christoph Wild, 110–18. München: Kösel Verlag, 1973.

Jackson, Frank. *Conditionals.* Oxford: Oxford University Press, 1991.

Kahneman, Daniel, and D. T. Miller. "Norm Theory: Comparing Reality to Its Alternatives." *Psychological Review* 93 (1986): 136–53.

Kant, Immanuel. *Critique of Pure Reason.*

Kröner, Franz. *Die Anarchie der philosophischen systeme* (Verm. u. verb. Nachdr. d. 1929 in Leipzig ersch. Ausg. Photomechan. Nachdr.) Geleitw. zur Neuausg.: Ferdinand Gonseth. Nachw.: "Über die Systematologie": Georg Jánoska; rept. (Graz: Publisher, 1970).

Kvart, Igal. *A Theory of Counterfactuals.* Indianapolis: Hackett, 1986.

Laertius, Diogenes. *Lives of the Eminent Philosophers.*

Levi, Isaac. *For the Sake of Argument.* Cambridge: Cambridge University Press, 1996.

Lewis, David K. "Counterfactual Dependence and Time's Arrow." *Nous* 13 (1979): 57–91.

———. *Counterfactuals.* Cambridge, MA: Harvard University Press, 1973.

———. "Probabilities of Conditionals and Conditional Probabilities." *Philosophical Review* 85 (1976): 297–315, 581–89.

Lycan, William G. *Real Conditionals.* Oxford: Clarendon Press, 2001.

Macksey, Kenneth, ed. *The Hitler Options: Alternate Decisions of World War II.* London: Greenhill, 1998.

———. *Invasions: The Alternate History of the German Invasion of England, July 1940.* London: Greenhill, 1999.

Marcos de Pinotti, G. E. "Aporías del no-ser y aporías de lo falso en 'Sofista' 237b–239c." *Revista Latinoamericana de Filosofía* 17 (1991): 259–74.

Matthews, Gareth B. *Socratic Perplexity and the Nature of Philosophy.* Oxford and New York: Oxford University Press, 1999.

McLaughlin, Robert. *On the Logic of Ordinary Conditionals.* Albany: State University of New York Press, 1990.

McTaggart, J. M. E. *Studies in the Hegelian Dialectic.* 3 vols. Cambridge: Cambridge University Press, 1922.

Mill, John Stuart. *Autobiography.*

Mondadori, Fabrizio, and Adam Martin. "Modal Realism: The Poisoned Pawn." *Philosophical Review* 85 (1976): 3–20.

Mott, André, Christian Rutten, and Laurence Bauloye, eds. *Aporia dans la philosophie grèque des origens à Aristote.* Louvain-la-Neuve: Traveaux du Centre d'Études Aristotelicennes de l'Université de Liège, 2001.

Niquet, Marcel. *Transzendentale Argumente: Kant, Strawson, und die Detranscendentalisierung.* Frankfurt am Main: Suhrkamp, 1991.

Plato. *Euthydemus.*

———. *Protagoras.*

————. *The Sophist.*

Pollock, John L. *Subjunctive Reasoning.* Dordrecht: D. Reidel, 1976.

Polsby, Nelson W., and Paul Seabury, eds. *What If? Explorations in Social Science Fiction.* Lexington, MA: Lewis Publishing, 1982.

Prantl, Carl. *Geschichte der Logik im Abendlande.* 3 vols. Leipzig: Herzel, 1855.

Quine, W. V. O. "On What There Is." *Review of Metaphysics* 2 (1948): 21–38.

Ramsey, F. P. "Law and Causality." In *Foundation Essays in Philosophy, Logic, Mathematics and Economics,* ed. D. H. Mellor. London: Routledge & Kegan Paul, 1978.

Rescher, Nicholas. "Belief-Contravening Suppositions." *Philosophical Review* 70 (1961): 176–96.

————. *Cognitive Harmony.* Pittsburgh: University of Pittsburgh Press, 2005.

————. *The Coherence Theory of Truth.* Oxford: Clarendon Press, 1973.

————. *Conceptual Idealism.* Oxford: Basil Blackwell, 1973.

————. *Conditionals.* Cambridge, MA: MIT Press, 2007.

————. "Counterfactuals in Pragmatic Perspective." *Review of Metaphysics* 50 (1996): 35–61.

————. *Dialectics.* Albany: State University of New York Press, 1972.

————. *Epistemetrics.* Cambridge: Cambridge University Press, 2006.

————. "The Fallacy of Respect Neglect." *Philosophy and Phenomenological Research* 71 (2005): 392–98.

————. *Hypothetical Reasoning.* Amsterdam: North Holland, 1964.

————. *Imagining Irreality.* Chicago: Carus Publishing Co., 2003.

————. *Paradoxes.* Chicago: Open Court, 2001.

————. *Philosophical Dialectics.* Albany: State University of New York Press, 2006.

————. *Plausible Reasoning.* Assen: Van Gorcum, 1976.

————. *Presumption and the Practices of Tentative Cognition.* Cambridge: Cambridge University Press, 2006.

————. *The Strife of Systems.* Pittsburgh: University of Pittsburgh Press, 1985.

————. "Thought Experimentation in Presocratic Philosophy." In *Though Experiments in Science and Philosophy,* ed. Tamara Horowitz and Gerald J. Massey, 31–41. Lanham, MD.: Rowman & Littlefield, 1991.

————. "Ueber einen zentralen unterschied zwishen theorie und praxis." *Deutsche zeitschrift fuer philosophie* 47 (1999): 171–82.

————. *What If: Thought Experimentation in Philosophy.* New Brunswick, NJ: Transaction Publishers, 2005.

Rescher, Nicholas, and Robert Brandom. *The Logic of Inconsistency.* Oxford: Blackwell, 1979.

Roese, N. J., and J. M. Olsen. "Self-Esteem and Counterfactual Thinking." *Journal of Personality and Social Psychology* 65 (1993): 199–206.

Ross, W. D. *Metaphysical Aporia and Philosophical Heresy*. Albany: State University of New York Press, 1989.

Sahlin, Nils-Eric. *The Philosophy of F. P. Ramsey*. Cambridge: Cambridge University Press, 1990.

Sanford, David H. *If P, Then Q: Conditionals and the Foundations of Reasoning*. London: Routledge, 1989.

Schneider, E. F. "Recent Discussions of Subjunctive Conditionals." *Review of Metaphysics* 6 (1952): 623–47.

Siitonen, Arto. *Problems of Aporetics*. Helsinki: Academia Scientiarum Fennica, 1989.

Sobel, Robert. *For Want of a Nail: If Burgoyne Had Won at Saratoga*. London: Greenhill, 1997.

Stalnaker, Robert C. "A Theory of Conditionals." In *Studies in Logical Theory*, American Philosophical Quarterly Monograph Series, No. 2, 98–112. Oxford: Blackwell, 1968.

Thines, Georges. *L'aporie*. Bruxelles: A. De Rache, 1968.

Thomsen, Brian, and Martin H. Greenberg, eds. *Alternate Gettysburg*. New York: Berkeley Books, 2002.

Tsouras, Peter. *Disaster at D-Day: The Germans Defeat the Allies, June 1944*. London: Greenhill, 2000.

———. *Gettysburg: An Alternate History*. London: Greenhill, 1997.

Walton, Douglas N. *Argumentation Scheme for Presumptive Reasoning*. Newark, NJ: Laurence Erlbaum Associates, 1996.

Whately, Richard. *Elements of Rhetoric*. London and Oxford: Oxford University Press, 1828.

William of Heytesbury. *Regulae solvendi sophismata* (ca. 1335).

Woods, Michael, David Wiggins, and Dorothy Edgington. *Conditionals*. Oxford: Clarendon Press, 1997.

INDEX OF NAMES

Schilpp, P. A., 149n10
Schneider, E. F., 144n2, 144n4, 157
Sextus Empiricus, 5, 142n1
Siitonen, Arto, 157
Sobel, Robert, 148n2, 157
Socrates, 103, 119, 125
Spinoza, 103–04, 150n11, 150n2
Stalnaker, Robert, 50, 53–55, 58–59,
    61–63, 144n6, 145n3, 146n6,
    146n11, 147n20, 157

Thales, 129
Theaetetus, 125
Thines, Georges, 157

Thrasymachus, 7, 103
Tsouras, Peter, 148n2, 157

Ullman-Margalit, Edna, 142n8

Walton, Douglas N., 143n8, 156
Weinberg, Stephen, 151n1
Whately, Richard, 143n8, 157
Wiggins, David, 157
William of Heytesbury, 150n10, 157
Woods, Michael, 157

Zeller, Eduard, 141n3
Zeno of Elea, 84, 120, 122